D0067886

ASK FOR THE OLD PATHS

By Abbie Tuttle

Thus saith the Lord, Stand ye in the ways, and see, and ask for the old paths, where is the good way, and walk therein, and ye shall find rest for your souls....

Jeremiah 6:16

© Copyright 1993 – Abbie Tuttle

All rights reserved. This book is protected under the copyright laws of the United States of America. This book may not be copied or reprinted for commercial gain or profit. Short quotations or occasional page copying for personal or group study is permitted and encouraged. Permission will be granted upon request.
Unless otherwise identified, Scripture quotations are from The King James Version of the Bible.

Take note that the name satan and related names are not capitalized. We choose not to acknowledge him, even to the point of violating grammatical rules.

Companion Press
P.O. Box 310
Shippensburg, PA 17257-0310

"Good Stewards of the
Manifold Grace of God"

ISBN 1-56043-609-3

For Worldwide Distribution
Printed in the U.S.A.

Contents

Dedication

To the Memory of
J. Edgar Hughes,
Teacher and Evangelist
1910-1989

Edgar was my cousin, my teacher, my mentor. Active in fields of ministry for almost sixty years, he taught me very early to appreciate the high value of the written Word of God.

Appreciation

I would like to express the special thanks to those who carefully read and critiqued the manuscript. Although busy in the work of their ministries, they willingly shared their time and energy to encourage me in this work. They are: Leonard Cook, Brent and Vicki Gilliland, Douglas Kline, and James White

Introduction

I recently read a haunting description of a spring which had once rushed clear and clean, with life-giving water.

> Years of rain seeping through a mound of sawdust had turned the water brackish. The spring itself was full of leaves, abandoned and diminished. She cleaned out handfuls of the leaves, down to the sandy bed, and waited for the water to flow clear again. The trickle came so slowly she could hardly believe this was the bold, fine spring she had once dipped into with deep buckets. (*The Tall Woman*, by Wilma Dykeman. Holt, Rinehart and Winston, 1962).

The description reminded me of our search for the old paths. The following pages reflect intense questioning.

What is the church? What was its origin?

What is a preacher? What is the message?

What are gifts of the Holy Spirit and their functions?

What is the "ministry of the saints?"

What should be the role of leadership?

What kind of government did the early church have?

Why was that government changed?

Can we expect persecution?

What should we do about all this?

Those who are drawn to the Lord by His Spirit come with many questions. Suddenly they experience a hunger to learn everything at once, and many times do not know where to begin. We will attempt to answer questions and close information gaps. The book can be read by an individual or studied together in a group.

We will read the account of the church's miraculous birth, growth and development in the books of Acts. We will receive further revelation of her function in the letters of the Apostles to the churches. We will learn of her later history and her glorious future.

There are many "churches" in existence today: local, national and international, all saying, "I am of Christ...." They are found with many labels, in all types of buildings and organizations. Some gather in storefronts, some in brick and stone with steeples, but all claim a connection to Christ, usually through a specifically identified founder. Many of these have little agreement and/or fellowship with each other.

The Holy Spirit is at work during these end-times, bringing people to the Lord from all walks of life, from all types of congregations, and from many different backgrounds. Many come with no concept of the Church as the Body of Christ. Most think of the church as a particular building furnished in a particular manner, in which one places one's body for an hour or so weekly.

Paul wrote to the Corinthian church about the dangers of making unwise comparisons among ourselves. We must be aware of the measure of the rule which God has given us. Consider Paul's warning:

> *For we dare not make ourselves of the number, or compare ourselves with some that commend themselves: but they measuring themselves by themselves, and comparing themselves among themselves, are not wise.*
>
> *But we will not boast of things without our measure, but **according to the measure of the rule which God hath distributed to us**, a measure to reach even unto you.*
>
> II Corinthians 10:12,13.

If God has given a measure of rule for the church, what is it? Many, realizing the urgency of the hour, are searching for answers. They are finding only confusion in the smorgasbord of churches, fellowships, organizations, with radio and TV adding to the mix.

If we sincerely want to know what God had in mind when He began the formation of the church, how do we find out? We look for *His measure of rule* from His word. He has carefully spelled out His desires for His body, the church. With dedication, we can learn those desires and follow the guidelines for conforming to His will.

The purpose of this book is to search His word for a pathway back to His will for His Church, so that there is no doubt about our direction. When opinions and methods increase to the point of confusion, it is time to follow God's advice through Jeremiah and "Ask for the old paths, where is the good way, and walk therein...."

How do we find the old paths? The specifications for His mighty living organism, the Church, were given clearly in the Scriptures. Have we fulfilled these specifications? Are we fulfilling them now?

Are we ready to clean out the debris which has clogged the spring for generations? If we examine our own perceptions, sincerely questioning their origins, many long-held opinions may be changed. This in turn will prove disruptive to some present day traditions. Many have grown accustomed to the shape of the "leaves" and "sawdust" without realizing that a pure flow of life-giving water is available if we clean out the debris.

We can follow the old paths, clearing out accumulated underbrush and wild growth as we go along, discovering His original plan for His church. It is our work to do. We have a *Guidebook*–the Scriptures. If we follow its leading and purge ourselves from everything interfering with His purpose, we will come to His destination. We will be vessels of honor, ready for the Master's use.

Abbie Tuttle

Group Discussion

Introduction

The theme verse for the book is taken from the prophet Jeremiah's message against Jerusalem (Jeremiah 6:16).

1. What was the condition of Jerusalem which caused the Lord's wrath? (Verse 7)
2. Is there a comparison with present-day world conditions?
3. What was the response of the people of Jerusalem to Jeremiah's warning? (Verse 10)
4. As a result of their response, what was the prophecy of Jeremiah? (Verses 11-15)
5. Still the Lord made an appeal (verse 16). What was their reply? (Verse 17)
6. After all the warnings and appeals, what was the word of final judgment? (Verses 18,19)
7. Is there a lesson for us from Jeremiah?
8. Read II Corinthians 10:12,13 and discuss the passage.

Chapter One

What Is a Preacher?

And He said unto them, Go ye into all the world, and preach the gospel to every creature. He that believeth and is baptized shall be saved; but he that believeth not shall be damned. And these signs shall follow them that believe; in My name shall they cast out devils; they shall speak with new tongues; they shall take up serpents; and if they drink any deadly thing, it shall not hurt them; they shall lay hands on the sick, and they shall recover.

Mark 16:15-18

The routine announcements of weekly services in present-day Bible-believing churches sound something like this: "Wednesday evening: Bible study and/or prayer meeting; Sunday morning: Sunday school and worship service; Sunday evening: evangelistic service. Gospel preaching. Invite your friends to come hear the gospel."

So...what's wrong with that? Consider that after the church was formed on the day of Pentecost, believers never met together to hear the gospel preached! Analysis of the purposes of their frequent gatherings show that they met:

> To receive teaching in the apostles' doctrine...for fellowship and prayer...to break bread together... on occasion of persecution...for problem solving... to hear prophetic messages...to send out apostles... to hear exhortation and admonition...for confirmation of churches...to establish leadership...to hear reports on apostolic missions...to settle issues of controversy...to correct incomplete knowledge...to hear reading of epistles...to receive encouragement.

They met together for many reasons, but they never assembled to hear an evangelistic sermon with an appeal to receive Christ. An "altar call" was never heard in a first century church gathering.

This leads to another question. Several ministries are listed as Christ's gifts to the Church: apostles, prophets, evangelists, pastors and teachers. Why is no ministerial office listed for the *preacher*? Some form of the word "preach" appears over 100 times in the New Testament. Paul considered himself a preacher first, even before his position as an apostle (I Timothy 2:7).

What is the definition of *preacher*? According to both Hebrew and Greek definitions, a preacher is a "heralder of divine truth, one who speaks of, proclaims thoroughly, and tells abroad that truth."

For many centuries, the preacher has been considered one who speaks from an elevated pulpit to listeners seated in pews before him. We assume that he has been divinely called for that purpose and trained for it as a profession.

We have missed the scriptural concept of preaching. Preaching is not a divinely appointed office, but a call to ministry of *every believer*. Careful study of Acts will show that indeed every believer was a preacher, telling forth the divine truth of Jesus' death, burial and resurrection, proving that He is alive by works done in His name. Those who accepted the message joined the body of believers and in turn preached to others. This was God's plan of expansion and it worked powerfully in the first century.

In every instance throughout the book of Acts, with one exception, preaching was addressed to groups or individuals *who had not previously heard the gospel.* The lone exception is Acts 20:7; in this case, the Greek word translated "preached" means "to discuss, reason, discourse."

Jesus' first ministry was preaching and healing. After He recruited and trained His disciples, He sent them out with instructions, "As ye go, *preach*, saying, The kingdom of heaven is at hand. *Heal* the sick, *cleanse* the lepers, *raise* the dead, *cast out* devils..." (Matthew 10:7,8). His followers' ministry was to be like His, and was not limited to the twelve. To one man who wanted to follow Him, He said, "Go thou and *preach* the kingdom of God" (Luke 9:60). The Gadaran delivered from demons wanted to follow Him and was told, "Go home to thy friends and tell them how great things the Lord hath done for thee..." (Mark 5:19).

Final instructions to His disciples before His ascension were, "Go ye therefore and teach all nations...to observe all things whatsoever I have commanded you..." (Matthew 28:19,20). He had trained them to *preach* and witness with *miracles*; now they were to teach others the same ministry. Was that ministry to continue into the twentieth century? Since He told them, "Lo...I am with you always, even unto the end of the world," we must assume that preaching with miraculous signs following should have continued, even to the present day.

Jesus promised them power to follow His instructions; they were to be fully equipped with His Holy Spirit and power to fulfill their mission. After the church received that power on the day of Pentecost, persecution arose. All Christians except the apostles scattered; the apostles remained in Jerusalem. How had the new believers been trained? "Therefore they that were scattered abroad went every where *preaching* the word" (Acts 8:4). They proclaimed the gospel wherever they went.

Philip was one of those men. He first went to Samaria "...and *preached* Christ unto them." Miracles supported his message, and the people believed. Then the Lord sent him to the desert for ministry to an Ethiopian official who needed help interpreting Isaiah. He "...opened his mouth, and began at the same scripture, and *preached* unto him Jesus" (Acts 8:35). From Philip's record, we know that preaching is not just directed to crowds, but also to individuals.

Immediately after Paul's conversion, "straightway he *preached* Christ in the synagogues, that He is the Son of God" (Acts 9:20). From his writings to the churches, we gain New Testament concepts of preaching and of those who should be doing it.

He wrote to "...all that be in Rome, beloved of God, called to be saints..." and quoted Isaiah. "How beautiful are the feet of them that *preach* the gospel of peace, and bring glad tidings of good things!" Paul was writing to laypeople and asked them, "...how shall they believe in Him of whom they have not heard?...and how shall they preach except they be sent?" (Romans 10:14,15). He was emphasizing their responsibility to preach the gospel.

Paul wrote the Ephesians, "...Take unto you the whole armour of God...your feet shod with the *preparation* of the *gospel* of peace" (Ephesians 6:13-15). Laypeople are to be prepared to take the gospel to others.

He also wrote the Philippians regarding some of their number who were preaching Christ from wrong motives: envy, strife, and contention. It didn't matter. "...Notwithstanding, every way, whether in pretence, or in truth, Christ is preached; and I therein do rejoice..." (Philippians 1:18). According to Acts 17, Paul spent less than a month in Thessalonica, but his letter to them reflects intense training.

> *For our gospel came not unto you in word only, but also in power, and in the Holy Ghost...and ye became followers of us, and of the Lord...so that ye were ensamples to all that believe in*

> *Macedonia...for from you sounded out the word of the Lord...in every place your faith to God-ward is spread abroad....*
>
> I Thessalonians 1:5-8

They were preachers! There is no reference to a specific "call" to preach; rather, preaching was the function of all who had accepted the gospel of the death, burial and resurrection of Christ.

Can the following statement be challenged from scripture?

> Preaching is to be done by every believer to those who have never heard the gospel, accompanied by healing and other miracles.

Down through the years, this pattern has been lost. After the first century, forms of worship evolved which led gradually to the preacher becoming an authoritative performer. Believers became an audience of spectators. They no longer sounded out the gospel, but expected the preacher to do it.

It is not too late for the twentieth century church to get back to the power and demonstration of the first century church. The same resources they received are still available to us. Do we now have them? Not in full power, although we have seen enough to know the possibilities.

Perhaps our search for the old paths will lead us back, prepared to "tarry until" we receive that power from on high. If the "fast food" and "instant everything" generation will dedicate themselves to prayer, fasting, and seeking the face of God, He will answer by fire. It follows that if the present-day church begins to function with the divine energy of the first century church, the same dynamic, rapid growth will result.

Search the Gospels, Acts and Epistles. See if these things are true. Are you ready to be challenged for such a ministry?

Group Discussion

Chapter One

1. In your advance study of this chapter, have you verified the purposes for the gathering of early believers? Discuss together the contrast between then and now.
2. Discuss the definition of "preacher" and relate it to believers today.
3. When Jesus instructed His disciples to go and preach (Matthew 10:7,8), what was included in that ministry?
4. How do we know that ministry was to continue even until today? (Matthew 28:20)
5. What was the believers' response to persecution? (Acts 8:4) Were these apostles or laypeople?
6. Should laypeople of today be preachers?
7. With a comparatively short time in Thessalonica, Paul had developed ministry among the people. How did he later describe them? (I Thessalonians 1:5-8)
8. How can we get back to the zeal and power of the early church?

Chapter Two

Jesus' Discipleship Training

...Go and make disciples of all nations...teaching them to obey everything I have commanded you.

Matthew 28:18-20, NIV

The four gospels record the complete story of Jesus recruiting and training His followers for their ministry. He patiently worked with them for over three years, teaching, correcting, giving instruction, showing by word and example how they were to make other disciples.

There is little emphasis on discipling today. Those interested in ministry are required to go to Bible School or College to train for a certain number of years. They sit in a classroom listening to "experts" telling them how to become a preacher, pastor or evangelist.

Why do we think we can improve on Jesus' methods? We have been presumptuous in substituting our own ways for building and leading the body of Christ.

Priority One For Discipleship

Jesus proved Himself before He began to minister and recruit others. "Full of the Spirit" after His baptism at Jordan, He was led immediately to the wilderness for testing. He emerged "in the power of the Spirit" and began reaching out to others (Luke 4:1-15). Note that He was *full* of the Spirit going into the wilderness, but returned in the *power* of that Spirit. He had overcome His enemy, and immediately began advancing the kingdom by preaching and healing.

Training For Service

> *And He ordained twelve, that they would be with Him, and that He might send them forth to preach.*
>
> Mark 3:14

Jesus needed them to be with Him, and He needs us today, not only for fellowship but also to send us forth to preach. As we join Him, we begin to learn His word, to tell others, and work in His kingdom.

Are we disciples of the Lord? Andrew was one of the first, and immediately brought others to Jesus, including his brother, Peter. Are we bringing others to the Lord, as Andrew did?

The disciples watched Him in action as they toured the countryside. They saw Him do various kinds of healings. Lepers were cleansed with a touch; the centurion's servant was healed with a word; Peter's mother-in-law was raised from a fever; demons were cast out at His command. They marveled when He took authority over the winds and sea. He challenged them, "Why are ye so fearful, O ye of little faith?"

After a time of observing His works, He gave them a special endowment of power for healing and against demons. He told them to expect persecution, but not to fear anyone except God. Others might kill the body, but only He could destroy both soul and body in hell.

They returned from their evangelistic tour, excited at what they had done and taught. "Even the devils are subject to us through Thy name!" He warned them that their rejoicing was misplaced. Rather, they were to rejoice that their names were written in Heaven. He pointed them to eternity.

Then He said, "Come ye yourselves apart into a desert place and rest while." He knew they needed relaxation. They took a boat and went to a desert place, but before they could rest there was another lesson to learn. In the service of the Lord, one may have to sacrifice resting time to fill needs of others. The people had seen them leave and when they arrived, already a crowd had gathered. Jesus responded with compassion, not irritation, and began to teach them.

Relationship With Others

Jesus was very emphatic about earthly relationships compared to relationship with Him. While He was teaching the multitudes, He turned directly to the disciples and said:

If any man come to Me, and hate not his father, and mother, and children, and brethren, and

> *sisters, yea, and his own life also, he cannot be My disciple.*
>
> Luke 14:26

> *He that taketh not his cross, and followeth after Me is not worthy of Me. He that findeth his life shall lose it: and he that loseth his life for My sake shall find it.*
>
> Matthew 10:38

Every relationship, including one's own life, must be secondary to Him. If this commitment is not made, failure is inevitable. The words He taught them still apply. When we become His followers, we must count the cost of commitment. We are not joining a fraternity for fellowship; we're joining the army of the Lord. Our lives, both temporal and eternal, are at stake.

He also taught them right relationships with those who were not part of their group. They reported forbidding a man to cast out devils in Jesus' name "...because he followeth not with us." Jesus said, "Forbid him not: for he that is not against us is for us." Shortly after that, a village of the Samaritans would not receive them as they passed through on their way to Jerusalem, and the disciples wanted to call down fire from Heaven to consume them. Again He was stern. "Ye know not what manner of spirit ye are of..." (Luke 9:49-55). Followers of Jesus still need this lesson.

Jesus reserved His most vitriolic scorn for the hypocritical scribes and Pharisees. He cautioned His disciples to have respect for the office and for the words of Moses they taught, but not to follow their hypocritical ways. People who think of Jesus as "gentle, meek and mild" should review His encounters with the Pharisees. He accused them of being blind guides, of caring for gold and silver, of being like sepulchres, making the outside look good while the inside was full of dead men's bones and uncleanness. He called them serpents and vipers! He had utmost compassion on sinners and the poor, but none for the hypocrite.

Importance Of The Word And Prayer

The Word of God is vitally important to the disciple. Jesus said to early believers, "...If ye *continue in My word* then are ye My disciples indeed" (John 8:31). A working knowledge of His word is essential for ministry. "If ye abide in Me, and My word abide in you, ye shall ask what ye will, and it shall be done unto you" (John 15:7). Time spent in the Word will show us the path of faith back to His promises, bringing answers to prayer.

Jesus taught His disciples to pray, both by example and by His word. He prayed with them, and gave them a prayer pattern which encompasses every facet of life: opening and closing with praise for God; asking for His will to be done in earth as in Heaven; requesting basic needs: invoking forgiveness; asking help against the enemy.

As disciples, we gain knowledge and strength through His Word and prayer, then recruit and teach others. Every member of the body of Christ can share with others what we have learned. Great depths of knowledge are not necessary to reach out and tell others what we have learned about the Lord. The writer to the Hebrews rebuked the saints for falling short in teaching. "...When for the time ye ought to be teachers, ye have need that one teach you again which be the first principles of the oracles of God..." (Hebrews 5:12). We are to be students of the Word, diligent in prayer, sharing with others as we learn.

Abiding In Jesus

There must be a fruit-bearing relationship with our Lord. It is called *abiding*. He told the disciples:

> *Abide in Me, and I in you. As the branch cannot bear fruit of itself, except it abide in the vine; no more can ye, except ye abide in Me. I am the vine, ye are the branches: He that abideth in Me, and I in him, the same bringeth forth much fruit: for without Me ye can do nothing.*
>
> John 15:4,5

The natural vine draws up nourishment from the ground through its root system, and sends it out through the branches. Jesus is the Vine; we are the branches, totally dependent on Him for our fruit-bearing ability.

Only through this abiding relationship with Jesus will His ministry be manifested through His disciples. In this scripture, bringing forth fruit signifies *action* "...For without Me ye can do nothing." What are we to be doing? We are to witness, proving that Jesus is alive by manifesting His life to others, with believer signs following.

As we abide in Him, His Spirit through us will lead others into the same relationship. Why did great crowds of people follow Jesus? He manifested the power and Spirit of His Father, reaching out to fill their needs. As He did these things, He was teaching His disciples by example. We are still to do this. "Be ye followers of me, even as I also am of Christ" (I Corinthians 11:1).

"The Greatest Of These Is Love"

"By this shall all men know that ye are My disciples, if ye have *love one to another*" (John 13:35). Love in our daily walk is the identifying criterion of the genuine disciple of Jesus. Without that love, we "...become as sounding brass, or a tinkling cymbal."

All manifestations of power, fruits and gifts of the Spirit are given to serve here on earth. *Love* is eternal and given for both this life and the next. The love of God expressed through us to others will authenticate our ministry. Jesus prayed just before His death on the cross,

> *...that the world may know that Thou...hast loved them, as Thou hast loved Me...that the love wherewith Thou hast loved Me may be in them, and I in them.*
>
> John 17:23,26

Sometimes our patience is tried by people we are discipling, but we have no excuse to give up. Jesus had problems with His disciples' lack of understanding, and sometimes rebuked them. "Oh, ye faithless and perverse generation...ye know not what manner of spirit ye are of...." We must continue to love, even as He loved those He was trying to teach.

Final Instructions

After three and one-half years of intensive training, it was time for Him to fulfill the purpose for which He was born. "...For this cause came I unto this hour." He was aware that they would forsake Him, but He looked beyond that dark hour and prayed both for them and for those who would believe on Him through their word.

After His resurrection, He met with them and gave further teaching. He gave them the commission to go into all the world, and with that commission, He gave them powerful signs to authenticate their ministry.

> *...Go ye into all the world, and preach the gospel to every creature. He that believeth and is baptized shall be saved; but he that believeth not shall be damned. And these signs shall follow them that believe; in My name shall they cast out devils; they shall speak with new tongues; they shall take up serpents; and if they drink any deadly thing, it shall not hurt them; they shall lay hands on the sick, and they shall recover.*
>
> Mark 16:15-18

Analysis of this passage shows that they were directed to go into all the world and preach. As a result, there would be baptized believers who would be empowered to minister with specific signs following their efforts: power over demons; new tongues; power over poisonous creatures and deadly things; power to heal the sick. The record of Acts shows that all these signs were manifested in the church.

With forty days of teaching after His resurrection, they were still looking for an earthly kingdom. They did not fathom the eternal meaning of the events which had occurred. He said, "It is not for you to know...." They would not understand until they received the Spirit.

Jesus' last instructions did not tell them to go into the cities and hold great crusades, form organizations, conduct seminars, or build church buildings and colleges. He told them simply to make disciples.

They were to go into all the world and preach the gospel, making disciples and training them; "teaching them to observe all things whatsoever I have commanded you...." They were to pass on His teachings and His works. Those who believed on Him through *their* word would continue His works in His name. Repentance and remission of sins would be preached in His name among all nations, beginning at Jerusalem (Matthew 28:19; Mark 16:17,18; Luke 24:47).

All these things they were to do, but not until they received the Holy Spirit.

> *...wait for the promise of the Father...ye shall receive power after that the Holy Ghost is come upon you: and ye shall be witnesses unto Me both in Jerusalem, and in all Judea, and in Samaria, and unto the uttermost part of the earth.*
>
> Acts 1:4-8

With these words He completed His earthly instructions. From this point on they would be directed by the

Holy Spirit whom He would be sending back to guide them in ministry.

> *...The Holy Ghost, Whom the Father will send in My name, He shall teach you all things, and bring all things to your remembrance, whatsoever I have said unto you.*
>
> John 14:26

New Disciples Receive and Use the Power of the Spirit

We who have believed on Him through their word have His Holy Spirit within us, an active force to teach and guide us through His Word so that we can in turn fulfill our ministry. Since He is our example, the first priority after our new birth is to learn to *use the power of the Spirit* in our own lives. He gives power to establish our life in Him, power to overcome every temptation of the enemy. As we overcome, we begin as He did, reaching out to others. We already know about the signs which He promised would follow.

Are you a born-again believer? Are these signs following you? If not, it's time to follow the old path to the Source for the power which enabled His first century disciples to carry out His word. His power was not removed from the earth at the death of the apostles, as some maintain. "Lo, I am with you always, even unto the end of the world." He is still with us.

The reason we see so little evidence of His power is because the church has failed to appropriate in faith the resources available in the Holy Spirit. Paul closed his prayer for the Ephesian church,

Now unto Him that is able to do exceeding abundantly above all that we ask or think, ***according to the power that worketh in us,*** *unto Him be glory in the church by Christ Jesus throughout all ages....*

Ephesians 3:20,21

Meditate on this prayer/statement. God is unlimited—He can do beyond all we ask or think. But He works *according to* (limited by) the power that works *in us*. The deficiency is not in Him—it is in us! We must search for the old path leading to more of His enabling power to witness that He is alive!

As Jesus' disciples were instructed to wait in Jerusalem to receive the promise of the Father, it is our duty to take time and effort to stay before the Lord to appropriate that power and see it begin working in us.

Verily, verily, I say unto you, he that believeth on Me, the works that I do shall he do also; and greater works than these shall he do, because I go unto My Father.

John 14:12

Group Discussion

Chapter Two

1. Jesus instructed His disciples to teach their converts everything He had commanded them. Discuss various things He had commanded them.
2. What should be our first priority before discipling others?
3. What were Jesus' instructions to the disciples when He sent them out?
4. What excited them most about their evangelistic tour?
5. Discuss Jesus' teaching to His disciples about relationships.
6. What place in ministry did the word and prayer hold?
7. Discuss the importance of abiding in Christ to any ministry and discipling of others.
8. What is the most important factor in letting the world know about Jesus Christ?
9. Discuss Jesus' final commission to the disciples (Mark 16:15-18). Was this ever withdrawn? Compare this with our present-day ministry.

Chapter Three

What is the Gospel Message?

Death, Burial, Resurrection

When they believed Philip preaching the things concerning the kingdom of God, and the name of Jesus Christ, they were baptized, both men and women.

Acts 8:12

Philip was not an apostle. In fact, he was one of those chosen by the congregation of the Jerusalem church to supervise distribution of food to widows. But when persecution forced believers to leave Jerusalem, "They...went every where preaching the word" (Acts 8:4). What did they preach?

Jesus had given His disciples their orders just before His ascension. "Go ye into all the world and preach the gospel to every creature" (Mark 16:15). What was that gospel?

The Good News

The total gospel message was that *Jesus, the Messiah, had come*, died as the *universal sacrifice for sin, was resurrected* after three days in a tomb, was *seated on His throne* in Heaven as our *Intercessor*, and would some day *return to earth*. The way to eternal life was now open to all humanity, both Jews and Gentiles, through His completed work.

They waited in Jerusalem for the promise of the Father, according to Jesus' word. That power totally changed them and furnished miraculous verification of their message that Jesus was alive.

Water and Spirit Baptism

On the day of Pentecost, after the Holy Ghost had filled them, Peter's message proved to his hearers that Jesus was Lord and Christ. The Holy Spirit convicted them and they asked, "What shall we do?" Peter did not answer, "Bow your head and repeat the sinner's prayer with me," then assure them that they were saved. He boldly told them,

> *Repent and be baptized, every one of you in the name of Jesus Christ for the remission of sins, and ye shall receive the gift of the Holy Ghost.*
>
> Acts 2:38

Three thousand responded to his message, and were baptized that same day! Contrast this with the present-day crusades held by prominent evangelists, when scores of people come forward to "accept the Lord as personal Savior," but are not instructed regarding water baptism or the gift of the Holy Spirit. It is not considered important enough to be a requirement, but on that first birthday of the church, "They that gladly received his word were baptized."

This was the message for both Jews and Gentiles. Those who believed that Jesus had come, died for humanity's sins and rose again, would become identified with Him in the death of repentance, burial of water baptism, and the resurrection life of His Holy Spirit. As believers increased and spread the word that Jesus was alive and working through His followers, the gospel spread outward from Jerusalem, as Jesus had commanded.

Paul later wrote to the Roman and Corinthian churches:

> *Therefore we are buried with Him by baptism unto death: that like as Christ was raised up from the dead by the glory of the Father, even so we also should walk in newness of life. For if we have been planted together in the likeness of His death, we shall be also in the likeness of His resurrection.*
>
> Romans 6:4-6

> *Moreover, brethren, I declare unto you the gospel which I preached unto you, which also ye have received, and wherein ye stand; by which also ye are saved, if ye keep in memory what I preached unto you, unless ye have believed in vain.*
>
> *For I delivered unto you first of all that which I also received, how that Christ died for our sins according to the scriptures; and that He was buried, and that He rose again the third day according to the scriptures.*
>
> I Corinthians 15:1-4

By the time Paul wrote these passages, the followers of Christ had received the message from Jesus, obeyed His command to wait for the power from on high, received that power, then began their ministry of spreading the gospel.

The message has not changed, and we are to be witnesses of that message, offering salvation to others. Every believer is to preach to unbelievers, as Jesus commanded.

> *And this gospel of the kingdom shall be preached in all the world for a witness unto all nations; and then shall the end come.*
>
> Matthew 24:14

Has the end come yet? Then every child of God should be preaching...heralding...telling forth. In our day, we may be preaching to those who are deceived by tradition-encrusted beliefs handed down through generations. They may have never heard the message as it was originally given. We must become expert in handling the Sword of the Spirit, which is the Word of God, so that in our preaching of the gospel message, we are able to cut through tradition with loving care and let the truth shine forth.

But will they believe us? When the Lord gave Moses a message for Israel, he had many doubts and questions. He was afraid they wouldn't believe him. God spoke to him, "What is that in thine hand?" The rod he carried became the instrument of divine power to perform miracles.

The Lord intended for signs and wonders to accompany His message wherever it was preached, and gave the disciples a list of the signs which would follow the believer. Power for these signs was given to them on the day of Pentecost and is still resident in the Holy Spirit Who indwells the believer. Signs are for the believer's ministry to be used in preaching the gospel. Just as the Lord gave Moses supernatural power to prove his message, so He gave power to His New Testament followers.

Over the centuries, His church has failed to maintain the manifestation of that power. It is time! We may have to return to the place of prayer and wait for a fresh infusion of His promised power, but it is there for those searching for the old paths.

He Will Return!

Don't forget the message that He will return! Many denominations have dropped this important feature of the message. They consider it a doctrine of "escape"—of avoiding the important matters of this life. By so doing, they are fulfilling one of the prophecies of the end time.

Peter wrote, "There shall come in the last days scoffers...saying, Where is the promise of His coming? For since the fathers fell asleep, all things continue as they were from the beginning of the creation" (II Peter 3:3,4).

The promise of His return was an important part of the apostles' message. Each New Testament writer mentioned it.

> PETER: *That the trial of your faith, being much more precious than of gold that perisheth, though it be tried with fire, might be found unto praise and honor and glory at the appearing of Jesus Christ.*
>
> I Peter 1:7

JAMES: *Be patient therefore, brethren, unto the coming of the Lord.*

James 5:7

JOHN: *Beloved, now are we the sons of God, and it doth not yet appear what we shall be, but we know that when He shall appear, we shall be like Him; for we shall see Him as He is.*

I John 3:2

JUDE: *Behold, the Lord cometh with ten thousands of His saints.*

Jude 14

PAUL: *For the Lord Himself shall descend from heaven with a shout, with the voice of the archangel, and with the trump of God: and the dead in Christ shall rise first.*

I Thessalonians 4:16

Each New Testament writer confirmed that the Lord would return. Don't neglect that part of the message, but be conscious that we have work to do in the meantime. Jesus said, "Occupy till I come." The word translated *occupy* means "actively doing business!" Our business is His work.

Group Discussion

Chapter Three

1. What was the total gospel message?
2. When was this first preached (Acts 2:14-39)? What was the response of the people?
3. How important was water baptism, from study of scripture references in this chapter?
4. How important should water baptism be today?
5. What was to accompany the message of the kingdom?
6. Review the words of each New Testament writer about the Lord's return.
7. What is the role of the body of Christ while waiting the Lord's return?

Chapter Four

Gifts of Men: The "Five-Fold" Ministry

When He ascended up on high, He led captivity captive, and gave gifts unto men...And He gave some, ***apostles****; and some,* ***prophets****; and some,* ***evangelists****; and some,* ***pastors*** *and* ***teachers****; for the perfecting of the saints for the work of the ministry, for the edifying of the body of Christ.*

Ephesians 4:8,11-12

When Paul listed Christ's gifts of men to the church, he named them and specified their purpose in the body. Every one of these offices includes, but is not limited to, preaching. These men were given for a specific purpose, according to the Greek text, "...For the perfecting of the saints *to* the work of the ministry."

The word *perfecting* means to "fit, prepare fully, restore, join together, completely furnish," in the sense of *equipping*. The word *ministry* means service, to *serve* or minister to others. The five offices of leadership are gifts of men from Jesus Christ to His Church, for a specific purpose: "For the perfecting (preparing, equipping) of the saints for the work of (their) ministry," for their serving of others. If this takes place according to instructions, the body of Christ will be edified, or built up. Men working in these leadership offices are trainers, coaches, to develop the believers into workers of high potential.

For reasons which can be identified in church history, leaders down through the generations have misinterpreted their own roles. They no longer see themselves as trainers or equippers of the saints. Ministry is reserved for the "clergy" class, with people as passive listeners. It is time to take the old paths back to re-examine the roles of leadership and their relationship to laity.

The leaders of the church are in the fullest sense gifts from Jesus Christ Himself, as we can see from the Ephesians passage. Each category of leadership has its place in the building up of the body of Christ, the Church. We will examine definitions of these ministries.

Apostles

Strong defines an apostle as a delegate, as an *ambassador of the Gospel*, someone *commissioned by Christ*, as a *messenger*, or one who is *sent*.

Jesus is the first "Apostle and High Priest of our profession" (Hebrews 3:1). Early in His earthly ministry, Jesus

"...called unto Him His disciples: and of them He chose twelve, whom also He named apostles" (Luke 6:13). He appointed them, trained them, and "...gave them power and authority over all devils, and to cure diseases. And He sent them to preach the kingdom of God, and to heal the sick" (Luke 9:1,2). We have no record of other apostles appointed during Jesus' earthly ministry. However, there are at least twenty-four apostles listed in the New Testament, so it is apparent that the Lord expected the office of the apostle to continue as one of the active leadership ministries for His church.

The first twelve hold a special place in Jesus' eternal plans. Their names are in the twelve foundations of the walls of the New Jerusalem (Revelation 21:14). After Judas' suicide and Jesus' ascension, the eleven convened a business meeting while they were waiting for the promise of the Father. Jesus had not instructed them to do this, but they chose Matthias to replace Judas by the process of casting lots. However, the result seems to have been ignored by the Lord; Matthias is never mentioned again. Later, Jesus personally intervened from Heaven to make His own choice, Saul of Tarsus. Paul referred to himself at least twelve times as an apostle called by Jesus Christ.

The book of Acts shows the apostles in action after the day of Pentecost. From this record we can learn the function of their office.

They preached the gospel in new areas, taught the believers who accepted the message, and ordained elders (presbyters) to oversee each local body (Acts 14:20-23).

They were in governmental authority. Another apostolic function was in the category of *government*, later listed in I Corinthians 12:28 as a gift. In the early days at Jerusalem, the rapid growth of the church brought problems of food distribution, and some widows were neglected. The apostles instructed the multitude of disciples, giving them guidelines, to choose for themselves people to take this responsibility. When these men were chosen, they were brought before the apostles for prayer and laying on of hands–the process we call "ordination." Their own main concern was expressed to "give ourselves continually to prayer, and to the ministry of the word."

There was no single "chief apostle." Paul made two references to "chief apostles" (always plural) in his writings, apparently referring to "them that were apostles before me" (Galatians 1:17). But there is no New Testament evidence for elevating one apostle with authority over the church. That deviation came later in Christian history.

Although Paul claimed the authority of an apostle, he did not use that authority to dominate the faith of others. He told the church at Corinth (II Corinthians 1:24), "Not for that we have dominion over your faith, but are helpers of your joy...."

Acts 15 relates how the apostles worked together in times of important decisions. Certain men from Judaea had visited Gentile churches and commanded that they be circumcised to be saved. Paul and Barnabas came from Antioch to meet with apostles, elders, and the Jerusalem church to consider the question of circumcision requirements for Gentile believers. Peter told his experience and opinion; Paul and Barnabas testified; James summarized and gave his recommendations. "Then pleased it the apostles and elders, with the whole church...." It was a group process, with brethren submitting to each other in the Spirit of the Lord.

They exercised judgment. When Ananias and Sapphira conspired to lie, Peter used apostolic authority in judgment. On another occasion, Paul commanded temporary blindness for a man who interfered with his ministry to one inquiring about the gospel.

They planted churches. As the gospel spread to many areas and word came back to Jerusalem, the apostles sent ministers to oversee, to bless and determine needs. After the persecution, many were scattered abroad as far as Antioch. "The hand of the Lord was with them: and a great number turned unto the Lord" (Acts 11:21). Barnabas was sent to Antioch to help them, and under his ministry, many people were added. He saw their need for teaching and went to Tarsus and brought back Saul. They assembled together for a whole year of teaching at Antioch.

The apostles operated in all the leadership ministries, as prophets, evangelists, pastors and teachers. Once the center of focus broadened beyond Jerusalem, they used these ministries in *church planting*. The Holy Spirit began to work through the church at Antioch to send forth apostles to spread the gospel to regions beyond. Local churches should still be sending messengers out!

Wherever churches were planted, they followed up by confirming the souls of the disciples, exhorting them to continue in the faith, emphasizing that there would be much tribulation ahead. They *ordained elders in every church* and prayed with fasting.

They worked as Jesus worked, training disciples who would in turn train others. Paul trained Timothy and Titus to set churches in order. He told Timothy, "The things that thou has heard of me...the same commit thou to faithful men, who shall be able to teach others also" (II Timothy 2:2). The objective of training was extension of the message and development of future leadership. As a result, the church grew rapidly.

They established discipline in the churches, dealing with various aspects of the Christian life to be lived "...not after the flesh, but after the Spirit." Paul wrote of the sanctity of the body as the temple of the Lord. Regulations for Christian marriage as well as the single life were made plain. Requirements were taught for fellowship at the table of the Lord, and disorder was rebuked. The spiritual gifts and their manifestation were taught, with regulation of their use in the local assembly.

The apostles, together with the prophets, form the foundation of the Church, with Jesus Christ as the chief corner stone. "...In whom all the building fitly framed together groweth unto an holy temple in the Lord..." (Ephesians 2:20-22).

If the apostolic office is restored to its rightful place, it will be an active, productive force in the body of Christ. Men of integrity, powerful in God, will be developed and sent out from local churches under the direction of His Spirit. They will aggressively spread the gospel of the kingdom and the name of Jesus Christ. They will plant and establish churches "...not where Christ was named..." (Romans 15:20). They will maintain the doctrine, directing the equipping of the saints, keeping the church steady and on course.

Prophets: From Whom the Message of God Springs Forth

The words of a true Old Testament prophet carried power, because God's message was springing forth. Elijah said to King Ahab, "As the Lord God of Israel liveth, before whom I stand, there shall not be dew nor rain these years, but according to my word" (I Kings 17:1). It happened!

New Testament prophets were second only to apostles in scriptural recognition. They are included in the foundation of the church. There is a spiritual *gift* of prophecy which Paul held in high esteem and encouraged everyone to covet, but the *office* of prophet was among Christ's gifts of leadership.

The contrast between the office and gift is illustrated in Acts 21:8-11.

> *We entered into the house of Philip...and the same man had four daughters, virgins, who did prophesy. And...there came down from Judaea a certain prophet, named Agabus.*

Philip's daughters prophesied, but Agabus was a prophet.

There were prophets in all the local assemblies of the early church. Three are named from the Jerusalem church: Agabus, Judas and Silas. There were prophets in the Antioch church, instrumental in ordaining and sending forth leaders.

The mysteries of Christ are revealed to the New Testament prophets.

Which in other ages was not made known unto the sons of men, as it is now revealed unto His holy apostles and prophets by the Spirit.

Ephesians 3:5

Prophets had an active part in the meetings of the saints. Paul gave them specific instructions.

Let the prophets speak two or three, and let the others judge....

I Corinthians 14:29

Prophets were to minister to the body, edifying, exhorting and comforting, training those who had received the gift of prophecy which Paul had told them to covet. Local assemblies heard from the Lord through the prophets, who were under submission to each other. Messages were subject to judgment of others for harmony with the Word.

Do we no longer need to hear directly from God by His Spirit? Would not each local assembly be blessed to have prophets among them? Some are awakening to the realization that these offices considered "obsolete" are needed now more than ever, and are seeking the Lord for their renewed manifestation. Another old path to search out!

Evangelist: One Who Proclaims Good News

We have learned that every believer is to be a preacher, telling forth the gospel to those who have not heard.

But there is also a leadership office of evangelist. They were to proclaim the gospel in new areas and train those called to that office. They were to train believers to become more effective preachers.

Very early in the development of the church, Philip preached as a layman to the Samaritans and to the Ethiopian official. Over twenty years later, when Paul stopped at Caesarea and visited his home, he is called, "Philip the evangelist." It had become his leadership office.

An evangelist speaks forth the gospel where Christ is not already known. Churches are planted as a result of his labors. His function among the saints is to help them become better preachers, not to hold "revivals." If all branches of leadership are functioning properly, with saints "working effectually," they won't need reviving, a word which is a reproach when used in connection with the church.

Pastors (Shepherds): Those Who Feed And Guide The Flock

Pastors were chosen from among the elders, presbyters, indicating maturity, and the office was plural, not singular. Vine's Greek Dictionary says they were raised up by the Holy Spirit, appointed as bishops or overseers to have the spiritual care of, and to exercise oversight of, the local churches. According to divine plan as seen in the New Testament, there were always several in each church for this important work. Oversight and authority were diffused among the elders.

When Paul called the elders of the Ephesus church to meet with him, his instructions defined their work.

> *Take heed therefore unto yourselves, and to all the flock, over the which the Holy Ghost hath made you overseers, to feed the church of God, which He hath purchased with His own blood.*
>
> Acts 20:28

As local churches were established, their bishops (pastors, overseers) and deacons were chosen from among the elders of the congregation. By the time Paul wrote his letter to the Philippian church, these had already been set in order. "...To all the saints in Christ Jesus which are at Philippi, with the bishops and deacons...."

After Paul was imprisoned, he delegated his authority to Timothy and Titus to work among the young churches, and we are blessed to have his instructions to them. He wrote:

> *...that thou shouldest set in order the things that are wanting, and ordain elders in every city....*
>
> Titus 1:5

Pastoral ministry is compared to that of a shepherd. The flock is nourished with the word of God. They are led into green pastures beside still waters. They are led in paths of righteousness through the valley of the shadow of death without fear of evil. They learn the rod and staff. They enjoy the table of fellowship. They receive overflowing blessings and are anointed and equipped for service. There is concern for stray sheep, as Jesus taught in His parable of the ninety and nine. The lesson illustrates active concern, not just passive waiting for the lost sheep to return.

Church history reveals that the office of pastor (mentioned only once in the New Testament) eventually became a supervisory, one-man position after emergence of very human lust for power over others. According to church historians, the second century saw rise and rule of one pastor in each congregation. The position of pastor became a salaried profession, giving administrative leadership to a passive audience. Thus began the hierarchy type of church government which has continued in various forms to the present.

In Matthew 18, Jesus first mentioned the church, giving principles of handling difficult problems of relationships within the flock. The powerful prayer of agreement, with principles of binding and loosing, are all in this chapter. Pastors were to apply these principles in guiding the flock.

Pastoral ministry is of paramount importance among gifts of men to the church, but it was not to be the CEO (chief executive officer) position which has evolved. Jesus identified personally with that ministry. "I am the Good Shepherd: the Good Shepherd giveth His life for the sheep" (John 10:11).

Teachers: Instructors of Truth in the Churches

Teaching is directed to disciples, believers. Paul sent Timothy to the Corinthians.

> *For this cause have I sent unto you Timotheus, who is my beloved son, and faithful in the Lord, who shall bring you into remembrance of my ways which be in Christ, as I teach every where in every church.*
>
> I Corinthians 4:17

Teachers were then, and still are, most necessary. The body of Christ needs to know and implement the great themes of Scripture. Not only was the teaching gift prominent, but believers were to become teachers. The writer to the Hebrews rebuked them for their deficiency.

> *When for the time ye ought to be teachers, ye have need that one teach you again....*
>
> Hebrews 5:12

Paul spent a great deal of his time teaching, both in person and by letter, as exemplified in I Corinthians 2:13.

> *Which things also we speak, not in the words which man's wisdom teacheth, but which the Holy Ghost teacheth, comparing spiritual things with spiritual.*

He stated the objective of teaching in Colossians 1:28:

> *...teaching every man in all wisdom: that we may present every man perfect in Christ Jesus.*

Combinations of Gifts

We observe that most leadership gifts are overlapping. Apostles are prophets, evangelists, overseers and teachers. Prophets can be evangelists and teachers. Pastoral work includes prophetic and teaching ministries.

Apostles, prophets and evangelists were itinerant ministries, moving from place to place. Pastors and teachers worked in the local church. When apostles returned to the churches they had planted, they spent time confirming and teaching them.

The five leadership offices, separate and combined, are for the equipping of saints for effective ministry. When the Lord's gifts of men furnish leadership according to His plan, and the saints cooperate in loving obedience, the body will be edified (built up) and the gospel will go forth to the ends of the earth. This is the divine plan for church growth and it worked marvelously in the first century.

Is present-day leadership ready to follow the old paths back to such a ministry?

Group Discussion

Chapter Four

1. What were the categories of leadership listed in Ephesians 4:8-12?
2. Why was "preacher" not included?
3. Discuss the specific purpose for these five ministries.
4. What was the meaning of the word "perfecting?"
5. Discuss the various aspects of the work of apostles and whether or not that position should still be in operation.
6. Discuss the work of prophets and whether or not that position should still be in operation.
7. Should the office of evangelist be to hold revivals of saints? If not, what is that ministry?
8. What is the primary function of pastors? Is there Biblical evidence for it being a singular position?
9. Discuss the purpose of teachers in the body of Christ as designated in Colossians 1:28.

Chapter Five

Gifts of the Spirit

*Unto the church of God...to them that are sanctified in Christ Jesus, called to be saints, **with all that in every place** call upon the name of Jesus Christ our Lord, both theirs and ours....*

*I thank my God always on your behalf...that in every thing ye are enriched by Him, in all utterance, and in all knowledge; even as the testimony of Christ is confirmed in you: **so that ye come behind in no gift**; waiting for the coming of our Lord Jesus Christ.*

I Corinthian 1:2,4-7

Notice that the above passage written by Apostle Paul to the Corinthian church is also addressed to "*all that in every place call upon the name of Jesus Christ.*" Does that include the church of this century? Since he admonishes us to "come behind in no gift, *waiting for the coming of our Lord Jesus Christ,*" obviously the word is for us today.

For in-depth research on gifts throughout the New Testament, read: Romans 12:1-8; I Corinthians, 12-14; Ephesians 4:7-13.

In Romans 12, Paul gives more insights on gifts and our attitudes in blessing others with them. He mentions waiting in patience, giving with simplicity to the necessity of others, ruling (administering) without slothfulness with diligence, unselfishly preferring others, showing mercy with cheerfulness, and kindly affection in brotherly love. All these attitudes reflect "serving the Lord" (12:11).

The Greek word for "gifts" is *charisms*, meaning "God's gifts upon believers by the operation of the Holy Spirit in the churches" (Vine).

Every person who has been born of the Holy Spirit is given the potential for one or more gifts of that Spirit. We can see by Paul's salutation to the Corinthian church (also addressed to us) that the gifts are part of our equipment for service. He lists nine in I Corinthians 12:8-10, each apportioned by the Spirit according to His will. They can be separated into three groups of three:

Inspirational Gifts -	Prophecy, tongues, and interpretation of tongues.
Power Gifts -	Faith, miracles, and the gifts of healing.
Revelation Gifts -	Discerning of spirits, word of wisdom and word of knowledge.

These are all available through the Spirit, and we are instructed to *covet earnestly* the best gifts. This implies a diligent effort on our part. As we seek the will of the Lord for the gifts He wants manifested in our lives, He will identify and develop them in us and we will be prepared for our ministry to the body of Christ.

> *The manifestation of the Spirit is given to every man to profit withal...but all these worketh that one and the selfsame Spirit, dividing to every man severally as He will.*
>
> I Corinthians 12:7,11

One who is seeking the will of the Lord for his gifts will prayerfully seek the Lord for direction; study the scriptures; enlist the help of leadership. As we have seen, it is their work to equip the saints for the work of the ministry. Through these resources, you can identify and develop your gift. The result will be obedient and powerful witnessing.

Paul wrote to Timothy, "Neglect not the gift that is in thee, which was given thee by prophecy, with the laying on of hands of the presbytery" (I Timothy 4:14). Later he admonished Timothy to "stir up the gift of God which is in thee." Not only are we to receive the gift with the help of leadership, but we are to keep it stirred up and share it with others.

Peter wrote, "As every man hath received the gift, even so minister the same one to another, as good stewards..." (I Peter 4:10).

Paul placed specific controls on the operation of vocal gifts in the assembly. Tongues were limited by the availability of an interpreter, and even then no more than three. Only two or three prophecies were to be given, with others judging the messages. Prophecy will never be in conflict with the revealed Word of God. "Let all things be done decently and in order."

As you study the book of Acts, you will see how these gifts were used. As a result, many were saved and the body of Christ was increased and edified. Peter used the gift of discernment of spirits in dealing with Ananias and Sapphira.

Another Ananias, a believer in Damascus, was used by God to bring Paul, who later became an apostle, into the church. As the result of Ananias' obedient ministry, we have a major part of our New Testament. With the healing of Aeneas at Lydda, "All that dwelt at Lydda and Saron saw him and turned to the Lord." When Dorcas was raised from the dead, "...it was known throughout Joppa: and many believed in the Lord." Do you see the connection between gifts and the growth of His church?

The gifts of the Spirit are powerful, which makes us realize the awesome requirement of a constant holy walk with the Lord. Let nothing come between you which would hinder the flow of His mighty power. When you realize the challenge of a life of service using His spiritual gifts as tools, you will see the emptiness of a lesser walk.

We shouldn't have to stop and repent of some light-weight foolishness to be ready to speak the word of authority and power for healing. It's a challenge! As a surgeon must be sterile to enter the operating room and wield the instrument of laser-light, so we must keep ourselves ready to use the instrument of Jesus' name in power and authority. This is true holiness!

There are people like Cornelius, perhaps some of your neighbors, who have received the Holy Ghost. God is pouring out His Spirit on all flesh in these days, among all kinds of churches. Don't downgrade their experience. Be reminded of Peter's statement:

> *Of a truth, I perceive that God is no respecter of persons: but in every nation he that feareth Him, and worketh righteousness, is accepted with Him.*
>
> Acts 10:34,35

There are people like those at Ephesus, who believed but had not heard about the Holy Ghost. Could you lead them into the life of the Spirit?

There are people like the Philippian jailer who may cry out, "What must I do to be saved?" They may have been given an incorrect answer, but don't cut them off. Use your gifts skillfully.

Remember Apollos? He was mighty in the scriptures but with incomplete knowledge. Aquilla and Priscilla, two laypeople, quietly instructed him "more perfectly."

Are you equipped to minister in situations like these? Have you become expert in handling the Sword of the Spirit, which is the Word of God, so that it does not kill? Peter wrote,

> *Sanctify the Lord God in your hearts: and be ready always to give an answer to every man that asketh you a reason of the hope that is in you....*
>
> I Peter 3:15

There are many hurting people, some of them close to you, to whom you can minister. In all situations of witnessing, you will be sensitive to the leading of the

Spirit. To someone complaining of illness, you might ask permission to pray for them. As the Spirit leads, you will pray with the authority of His name, and His power will be present to heal. You will have been a witness, and those who "...were ordained to eternal life" will believe.

With so little emphasis on gifts in today's churches, there is a need for in-depth research in the Word and dedicated prayer for restoration of the gifts to the ministry of laypeople. This may require effort on the part of those who see the need, especially if leadership is not cooperative. There are some in leadership who feel that supernatural ministry is not for today. But the Word is clear, and we have seen that it was written for the twentieth century as well as the first century.

When Paul instructed the church to "covet earnestly the best gifts," the command was as valid as any other in the New Testament. We are at fault if we neglect to ask the Lord in faith for His gifts. He has made His will plain in His Word; our work is to implement that word in our own lives.

Just before He ascended, Jesus gave instructions to His disciples about the power to be manifested through those who believe on Him. Are we fulfilling Jesus' prophecy by appropriating that power, using the gifts of His Spirit? This power for ministry descended on the church at Pentecost and its potential is resident in *every* Spirit-filled believer. As we witness to those who have not heard the good news, we can by faith minister in His supernatural power.

We must find the old paths back to this rich vein of ministry!

Group Discussion

Chapter Five

1. Are the scriptures pertaining to gifts of the Spirit applicable to the church today? How do we know?
2. There are nine gifts of the Spirit listed in I Corinthians 12:8-10. Discuss them under the headings of *inspirational gifts, power gifts, and revelation gifts*.
3. Are these gifts as prevalent among the body of Christ as they were in early church days? How can we see their restoration?
4. What were the limitations on the use of tongues and prophecy in early church gatherings?
5. Review additional gifts mentioned in Romans 12:1-8.
6. How does a life of holiness relate to the manifestation of the gifts of the Spirit?

Chapter Six

The More Excellent Way

With Paul's command to covet the best gifts, he said, "Yet show I unto you a more excellent way," then launched into one of the most beautiful chapters of the Bible, his essay on love, or charity. It is the centerpiece between his teaching on the gifts of the Spirit and the regulation of their use in the local assembly.

He emphasizes that the gifts–tongues, prophecy, mysteries of wisdom and knowledge, faith, giving–all fade into nothingness compared to the abiding love of God. All the gifts are given for kingdom use in this life. The character of love is for eternity.

Love is closely associated with the holiness of God. Notice its characteristics:

Charity suffereth long, and is kind; charity envieth not; charity vaunteth not itself, is not puffed

> *up, doth not behave itself unseemly, seeketh not her own, is not easily provoked, thinketh no evil; rejoiceth not in iniquity, but rejoiceth in the truth; beareth all things, believeth all things, hopeth all things, endureth all things.*
>
> I Corinthians 13:4-7

Paul had instructed the Ephesians to grow up in Christ, "...from whom the whole body fitly joined together and *compacted* by that which every joint supplieth...." What is the substance which *compacts* the whole body together? Paul gives us the answer in Colossians 3:14. "Put on love, which is the *bond* of perfection." There must be a flow of love between people and the leaders who are equipping and perfecting them. This flow of love will be evident in their dealings with each other. Edification and increase will result only if that compacting agent, love, is supplied by *every part*.

Holiness: Requirement For Effectual Work

The word *effectual* implies efficiency in production of desired results. Another analogy from Paul's letter to Timothy gives insight into God's expectation of us.

> *In a great house there are not only vessels of gold and of silver, but also of wood and of earth; and some to honour, and some to dishonour. If a man therefore purge himself from these, he shall be a vessel unto honour, sanctified, and meet for the master's use, and prepared unto every good work.*
>
> II Timothy 2:20,21

Watch for the word *work* in your studies. We are to be ready for the Master's use, purged of everything which might dishonor. It is a high calling. Note that *God* does not do the purging. We must *purge ourselves* from dishonor. Peter wrote that God has already given us in His Spirit *all things* necessary to accomplish this purging (II Peter 1:3). How do we make these things part of us?

> *...Through the knowledge of Him that hath called us to glory and virtue: whereby are given to us exceeding great and precious promises: that by these ye might be partakers of the divine nature, having escaped the corruption that is in the world through lust.*
>
> II Peter 1:3,4

To qualify for work in the body of Christ, to be a vessel suitable for His use, we must be partakers of His nature, having escaped the corruption of the lusts of the world. Consider the corruption which would bring dishonor and render us unfit for His service.

Satan's Clever Methods

Are you aware that all of satan's dealings with mankind come through three avenues?

> *For all that is in the world, the lust of the flesh, and the lust of the eyes, and the pride of life, is not of the Father, but is of the world.*
>
> I John 2:16

How does satan accomplish his victories?

> ***Every man is tempted when he is drawn away of his own lust and enticed. Then when lust hath conceived, it bringeth forth sin....***
>
> James 1:14,15

Satan cannot overcome us unless we give him permission by opening one of these avenues. Learn satan's methods of operation. He deceived Eve this way. She saw that the fruit was good for food (lust of the flesh), that it was pleasant to the eyes (lust of the eyes), that it was desirable to make one wise (pride of life). She was drawn away by her own lust, and fell into sin.

Satan tried the same tactics on Jesus. He tempted Him to make bread of stones (lust of the flesh). He showed Him all the kingdoms of the world (lust of the eyes), and challenged Him to do a spectacular, miraculous leap from the pinnacle of the temple (pride of life). Jesus defeated satan with resources available to the weakest member of the body: "It is written...." Knowledge of the Word of God is basic for an overcoming life. We must know His word if we are to be a vessel of honor, suitable for His use.

Satan has no new methods. The old ones have been quite successful enough. He can appeal through these three avenues, but he cannot overcome us unless we are "...drawn away of our own lust and enticed." Recognize satan as a seducer and deceiver who can only operate if we open the avenue of lust. It is our responsibility to know ourselves and to know our enemy. James further instructs, "Submit yourselves therefore to God. Resist the devil and he will flee from you" (James 4:7).

The directive is clear: *submit* to God and *resist* the devil. The promise follows—satan will flee. If your life is totally submitted to God in every respect, if you are filled with and walking in His Spirit, you have power in Jesus' name to resist the devil and walk in victory. Then you will be able to continue with Peter's instructions.

> *And beside this, giving all diligence, add to your faith virtue; and to virtue knowledge; and to knowledge temperance; and to temperance patience; and to patience godliness; and to godliness brotherly kindness; and to brotherly kindness charity.*
>
> II Peter 1:5,6

These pertain to life and godliness, which God has already given us in the Holy Ghost. But we must add them, making them part of ourselves. What happens when these have been added?

> *For if these things be in you and abound, they make you that ye shall neither be barren nor unfruitful in the knowledge of our Lord Jesus Christ.*
>
> II Peter 1:8

When this verse describes us, we're ready as vessels fit for the Master's use. We can then be used in the "effectual" working in the measure of every part to build His great house, the body of Christ.

> *And above all these things put on charity, which is the bond of perfectness.*
>
> Colossians 3:14

Group Discussion

Chapter Six

1. Discuss the fact that the gifts of the Spirit are given for our lives and ministries today, and do not extend into eternity.
2. What profound quality and characteristic of God are we to possess, both for time and eternity?
3. Discuss examples of the characteristics of love as given in I Corinthians 13:4-7, with examples of difficulties of manifesting these qualities.
4. Explain how love works in the body of Christ from Colossians 3:14.
5. How does the concept of holiness fit in with a study of love?
6. Through what three avenues does satan attack mankind? What defense do we have available? (James 4:7)
7. What are the characteristics we are to add to our faith, according to II Peter 1:5,6?
8. What happens when these have been added?

Chapter Seven

Saints: For the Work of the Ministry

In everything we have considered to this point, we have learned that *everyone* is to be a *preacher* and a witness to those who have not heard the gospel. We know that the *message* to be sounded out is that Jesus Christ came, died as our sacrifice for sin, was buried and arose again, giving eternal life to as many as believe on His name.

We have learned about Christ's *leadership* gifts of men for the purpose of equipping people for the work of *their* ministry, and that *gifts of the Spirit*, tools for service, are available to those who seek them earnestly. We know, too, that all ministry is to be done in *love*, without which it will be totally worthless.

We glimpse the beautiful synchronization possible in Paul's letter to the Ephesians:

From whom (Christ) the whole body fitly ***joined together*** *and* ***compacted*** *by that which* ***every joint supplieth****, according to the* ***effectual working*** *in the measure of* ***every part****, maketh* ***increase*** *of the* ***body*** *unto the* ***edifying*** *of itself in* ***love.***

Ephesians 4:16

From this passage we can see that the work to be done involves both leadership and laity.

What Is Effectual Work?

Everything we've considered *qualifies* us for work; what is that *work*? We know Jesus trained and equipped His disciples for the work of their ministry. He taught them to preach and to heal. He taught them the power of His Name.

Hitherto have ye asked nothing in My name: ask, and ye shall receive, that your joy may be full...at that day ye shall ask in My name....

John 16:24-26

He gave them the key to His power: they would have the authority of His Name. We still have that authority! He expected them to continue His works in the world and to teach future believers.

Verily, Verily, I say unto you, He that believeth on Me, the works that I do shall he do also; and greater works than these shall he do; because I go unto My Father.

John 14:12

Just before He left the earth, He gave them final instructions to teach all believers to obey the same things He had commanded them, and promised His presence with them until the end of the world. We have already seen that Mark 16:15-18 is the work of the believers, to be done through the power of the Holy Ghost, available since Pentecost.

> *Ye shall receive power, after that the Holy Ghost is come upon you; and ye shall be* ***witnesses*** ***unto*** *Me both in Jerusalem, and in all Judaea, and in Samaria, and unto the uttermost part of the earth.*
>
> Acts 1:8

They were given the *authority of His Name*, the *power of the Holy Ghost*, and the *command to witness*. Notice that He did not tell them to go out and save the world. That is not our commission. Our work is to labor as *witnesses* in the harvest field of wheat and tares, using the power of His Spirit by the authority of His Name.

Witnessing In the Early Church

Wherever the people preached and witnessed, the power of God was there to confirm the message with miraculous works. Stephen, a layman appointed to "serve tables" was full of faith and power and "...did great wonders and miracles among the people" (Acts 6:8).

When severe persecution arose against the Jerusalem church, believers left but continued to witness. They "...went every where preaching the word." Signs and wonders followed them. They were doing effectual work, and the body of Christ increased constantly. They were occupied in the ministry of the saints, witnessing in the power of God.

A pagan philosopher of the early centuries, an opponent of the gospel, wrote that Christians with little or no education seized every opportunity to witness to people, and even when confronted by educated people, they would not stop.

Key To Manifestation of Power

Peter described the healing of the lame man, "...His name through faith in His name hath made this man strong..." The name of Jesus must be used in faith for the power of the Holy Ghost to produce healing or other miracles. *Faith* must be developed as part of the equipment for ministry.

We are all familiar with the Presence of God as we praise and worship Him. There is great blessing and strength as we worship the Lord in Spirit. *But know this:* the Presence of God felt in a worship service is not necessarily power manifested. Think about that! We must learn the difference, and electricity provides an illustration.

If you touch an exposed electric wire, you will receive a "thrilling" charge of electricity. We may get such a physical thrill when we praise the Lord in prayer, singing, dancing. But these expressions are not His power manifested; they are our reaction to His Presence. If electricity is to accomplish productive work of lighting buildings or operating machinery, there must be more than a "charge." Electric power must be harnessed according to specific laws of electricity for productive operation.

So it is with the power of God. With the passage of centuries, many of the body of Christ have lost contact with the specific laws available to them for productive ministry. They have been satisfied with the thrill, not pursuing the quest for harnessing that great energy.

Faith is Basic

Fruitful ministry requires faith. Both leadership and people should concentrate on building faith. Paul told the Romans, "God hath dealt to every man a measure of faith." Peter said we are to add to that faith. How? "Faith cometh by hearing and hearing by the Word of God." We must have an insatiable appetite for the Word of God. Job expressed his hunger, "I have esteemed the words of thy mouth more than my necessary food" (Job 32:12).

Members of the body of Christ should share the Word with each other and with their leaders. A lively interchange of discoveries from the Word can be much more fascinating and rewarding than discussing politics or the economy. When the Word has become an integral part of our lives, we will be ready to operate in the realm of faith.

The Authority of the Believer

Every believer indwelt by the Holy Ghost, living an overcoming life in active faith, can take authority in Jesus' Name over sickness in themselves and in others. You will find no scripture proving that sickness and disease originate from God. They come from satan's effect on a fallen world. His power was broken at Calvary, but he is still an expert at deception. If he can deceive us successfully, he will put sickness and disease on us and make us believe we must accept them. Don't let him do it! Reject them in Jesus' Name! Satan can only work with our permission, but some of us cooperate with him. We talk about "my headaches...my backaches...my rheumatism" as though we were cherishing them. Don't give satan that satisfaction.

There is both negative and positive power in your spoken word. Jesus cautioned, "For by thy words thou shalt be justified, and by thy words thou shalt be condemned..." (Matthew 12:37). The body of Christ has help for those who need it. With anointing and prayer of the elders, we have the promise, "The Lord shall raise him up." Don't ask a person how he feels after anointing and prayer–just praise the Lord with him for his healing! Fight the devil with the Word and stand on it. Search the "great and precious promises" and use them!

Doubters will raise the question of Paul's thorn, looking for excuses to entertain illness without fighting back. The Lord told Ananias that Paul would suffer many things, and he did. He made a lengthy list of them in II Corinthians, but sickness was not among them. Others say, "Well, if I never got sick, I'd never die." Not true. Moses and Aaron both died at the Lord's appointed time, without sickness. When the Lord wants us, He can take us without long illness. When Moses died, "...his eye was not dim, nor his natural force abated." God is no respecter of persons, and we can operate in faith for good health. The key word here is *faith*. Jesus said, "According to your faith be it unto you" (Matthew 9:29).

Of course, we cannot abuse our bodies with wrong health habits, stuff ourselves with too much or the wrong kinds of food, and expect God to heal the consequences. That's lust of the flesh, not walking in faith. The fruits of the Spirit include temperance, which is moderation.

With victory over satan in our own lives, we can powerfully witness in deliverance for others. It is a high calling. People everywhere are looking for answers which the body of Christ should be furnishing. Are you ready for the ministry?

Witnessing in the Power of His Spirit Today

Every person has his own personal Jerusalem, Judaea and Samaria for expansion of ministry. It may be the office, the factory, the neighborhood, the school, or the street.

There are people who have never heard the message of Jesus' death, burial and resurrection and what it can mean in their lives. Be trained to tell them effectively.

Are you equipped to witness? Have you become expert in handling the Sword of the Spirit, the Word of God, so that it does not kill? Don't look scornfully on those who profess less than you think they should have. Use the gift of mercy. There are many hurting people who need the help you can furnish, if you're equipped.

> *Sanctify the Lord God in your hearts: and be ready always to give an answer to every man that asketh you a reason of the hope that is in you....*
>
> I Peter 3:15

Be sensitive to the leading of the Spirit in communicating with others. If you are led by the Spirit to pray for someone's healing, you will pray with the authority of the Name, and the power of the Spirit will heal. That's witnessing! If we're not operating in that realm yet, we must ask for help (the old paths) to reach that level.

As you seek the Lord, coveting earnestly the best gifts,

> *Let the word of Christ dwell in you richly in all wisdom; teaching and admonishing one another in psalms and hymns and spiritual songs, singing with grace in your heart to the Lord. And whatever ye do in word or deed, do all in the name of the Lord Jesus, giving thanks to God and the Father by Him.*
>
> Colossians 3:16

Study the Acts and Epistles to see how to become a productive part of the body of Christ. As the leadership works with the people to develop their ministries, with the believers cooperating in loving dedication, the body of Christ will reach out in manifestation of the Living Word,

> *...making increase unto the edifying of itself in love.*
>
> Ephesians 4:16

Group Discussion

Chapter Seven

1. Read together Ephesians 4:16, meditate on its meaning and discuss.
2. What is "effectual work"? Discuss in relation to Jesus' words in John 14:12.
3. By what authority can we do His work? (John 16:24-26).
4. Read the commission which Jesus gave His followers after His resurrection (Acts 1:8). What power would be given to do His work? What command did He give them?
5. Is the present-day church witnessing in the power and authority which Christ commanded? What can we do about appropriating those factors into our ministries?
6. Make specific suggestions dealing with these conditions.

Chapter Eight

Persecution

Remember the word that I said unto you, The servant is not greater than his lord. If they have persecuted Me, they will also persecute you; if they have kept My saying, they will keep yours also. But all these things will they do unto you for My name's sake, because they know not Him that sent Me.

John 15:20,21

Very early in His disciples' training, Jesus talked with them about persecution. His warnings have applied to the church down through the centuries, and even today His followers are suffering horrible persecution in parts of the world. But along with His warnings, He promised blessing.

Blessed are ye, when men shall revile you and persecute you, and shall say all manner of evil against you falsely, for My sake. Rejoice and be exceeding glad: for great is your reward in heaven: for so persecuted they the prophets which were before you.

Matthew 5:11,12

Why is persecution such a significant factor in the life of the Christian? It began with Cain against his brother, Abel, motivated by Cain's rebellion against making the proper sacrifice according to the Word of God. He substituted fruits of the cursed ground instead of a blood sacrifice, and God would not accept his offering. In murderous rage he struck out at Abel, whose offering of a lamb had been accepted.

The pattern of persecution is that those who diligently follow the Lord are persecuted by those who want to maintain their own ways. The prophets of Israel were killed by those who didn't want to hear the word of the Lord which commanded them to separate from their idolatry and wickedness.

Persecution should not be confused with the everyday problems and griefs that plague all humanity. The human condition of trouble and sorrow has been with us since the fall of Adam and Eve.

The persecution we are studying is inflicted with demonic hatred against those who are dedicated, effective servants of the Lord. It is especially strong against those who are ministering by the Holy Spirit with signs following, often imposed by those who claim status as people of God.

Persecution against Jesus began as soon as he started His ministry. This persecution came from the Pharisees who were very zealous in the law of Moses and all the traditions which had accumulated through the years.

They considered themselves holy and separate, superior to common people. There were political motives beside their zeal for the law. At their council with the chief priests, one said, "What do we? For this Man doeth many miracles. If we let Him thus alone, all men will believe on Him: and the Romans shall come and take away both our place and our nation" (John 11:47,48). In their political zeal for their "place and nation," they were relentless in their efforts to silence Jesus, and of course eventually crucified Him.

Jesus warned His disciples shortly before His death:

> *Then shall they deliver you up to be afflicted, and shall kill you: and ye shall be hated of all nations for My name's sake.*
>
> Matthew 24:9

After Jesus' resurrection and ascension, the young church immediately became the target of those who had persecuted Jesus. Scripture records the martyrdom of Stephen and later James. Because persecution intensified after Stephen's death, many believers scattered from Jerusalem and preached the gospel in new places. The New Testament writings confirm the prevalence of persecution. Peter and Paul as well as other leaders were martyred by the Romans during the first century. Roman emperors considered themselves gods and demanded allegiance. Many paid with their lives for refusing to worship Roman gods. In spite of persecution, the church continued to grow. Those who believed in Jesus and made the decision to follow Him knew their lives were at stake.

James

First of the apostles to die for his Lord, James was a member of the innermost circle with Peter and John, his younger brother. He had been present at the transfiguration. He could have witnessed the agony of Jesus' suffering in the Garden.

James and his brother John were surnamed, "Sons of Thunder." They were hotheaded, and Jesus rebuked them when they wanted to call down fire upon people of Samaria for not welcoming them. When he and his brother John desired a place at Jesus' right hand in the kingdom, Jesus asked if they were able to drink His cup. They said they could.

James was beheaded by King Herod Agrippa I, about 44 A.D. (Acts 12:1,2). So James fulfilled the prophecy of Jesus that he would drink of his Master's cup.

After the New Testament record is closed, we go to early church sources for information on subsequent persecution of the followers of Jesus Christ. The fiercest persecution came from Rome because the early Christians refused to worship Roman gods and emperors.

Peter

George Jowett, a London historian, wrote of Peter that he was "maliciously condemned, cast into the horrible, fetid prison of the Mamertine (Rome). There for nine months, in absolute darkness, he endured monstrous torture manacled to a post. How Peter managed to survive those nine long dreadful months is beyond human imagination. Yet, his magnificent spirit remained undaunted. It flamed with the immortal fervor of his noble soul proclaiming the Glory of God through His Son, Jesus Christ. In spite of all the suffering Peter was subjected to, he converted his jailers, Processus, Martinianus, and forty-seven others.

"He met his death at Rome at the hands of the murderous Romans who crucified him. He refused to die in the same position as our Lord, declaring he was unworthy. Peter demanded to be crucified in the reverse position, with his head hanging downward. This wish was gratified by the taunting Romans in Nero's circus, A.D. 67."

When we read the description of Peter's suffering, his admonition to the church becomes more meaningful:

> *Beloved, think it not strange concerning the fiery trial which is to try you, as though some strange thing happened unto you: but rejoice, inasmuch as ye are partakers of Christ's sufferings...if ye be reproached for the name of Christ, happy are ye....*
>
> I Peter 4:13,14

Andrew

He was first a disciple of John the Baptist, but after John introduced Jesus as the Lamb of God, Andrew, with Peter, Philip and John, started following Jesus. He is known as the disciple who brought others to Jesus.

Tradition has placed Andrew's ministry to the Scythians (part of modern southern Russia), to Byzantium, and to Greece. His martyrdom at Aichaia was recorded in a history written in the 15th century. The proconsul of Achaia, after debate, ordered Andrew to forsake his religion or be tortured fiercely. He urged Andrew not to lose his life; Andrew urged the proconsul not to lose his soul. He was crucified on an X-shaped cross, which is still described as "St. Andrew's Cross," the symbol of Scotland, a country which considers him their patron saint.

"After patiently bearing scourging, Andrew was tied, not nailed, to a cross, that his suffering might be prolonged. He exhorted the Christians and prayed. Some people importuned the proconsul, but Andrew besought the Lord that he might seal the truth with his blood. He died on November 30, 69 A.D."

John

Identified as "the disciple whom Jesus loved," John was the only one of the apostles to die a natural death. He took responsibility for Mary until her death. According to tradition, she died in Ephesus, where John spent many years.

He was not exempt from persecution. Exiled to the barren isle of Patmos, he wrote his Revelation of Jesus Christ. After some years, he was released from Patmos and returned to Ephesus, where he wrote his Gospel of John. Unproved legend says that he was boiled in oil but was miraculously delivered.

His own triumphant testimony says:

> *I John, who also am your brother, and companion in tribulation, and in the kingdom and patience of Jesus Christ, was in the Isle that is called Patmos, for the word of God, and for the testimony of Jesus Christ.*
>
> Revelation 1:9

He died at Ephesus around 100 A.D.

Philip

When Jesus recruited Philip, he said simply, "Follow me." He was from Bethsaida, the same city as Andrew and Peter. Immediately, Philip found his friend, Nathaniel, and brought him to the Lord.

According to early writings, Philip traveled to Scythia and ministered for twenty years, then came to Hierapolis in Phrygia. His preaching against the worship of a serpent there so angered them that they crucified him. "Being bound on the cross, they stoned him; thus he yielded up his spirit to God, praying, like his divine Master, for his enemies and tormentors." He is supposed to have been 87 at his death.

Bartholomew (Nathaniel) and Thaddeus

These two apostles were the traditional founders of the Armenian Church. Their tombs are shown and venerated in Armenia as sacred shrines.

One account says, "The popular traditions concerning St. Bartholomew are summed up in the Roman Martyrology, which says he 'preached the gospel of Christ in India; thence he went into Greater Armenia, and when he had converted many people there to the faith he was flayed alive by the barbarians, and by command of King Astyages fulfilled his martyrdom by beheading....'"

In "The History of the Armenian Church," the author says: "All Christian Churches accept the tradition that Christianity was preached in Armenia by the Apostles Thaddeus and Bartholomew in the first half of the first century, when the Apostles of Christ were fulfilling their duty in spreading the Gospel–in Jerusalem and all Judea and in Samaria, and unto the uttermost parts of the earth–(Acts 1:8). The generally accepted chronology gives a period of eight years to the mission of St. Thaddeus (35-43 A.D.) and sixteen years to that of St. Bartholomew (44-60 A.D.), both of whom suffered martyrdom in Armenia."

Following the Great Commission was costly for the Apostles! Could we qualify?

Thomas

According to the traditions of the Mar Thomar Syrian Church of South India, Apostle Thomas landed at Malabar, South Indiana in 52 A.D. In early church history there are many references to the fact that he instructed and baptized thousands of people, and ordained leadership in the churches for their spiritual needs.

One description of the churches of India relates that there were no special leaders, but all elders held equal rights in administering sacraments and burying the dead. Income was distributed equally among them.

The Brahmin people were resentful and envious at the success of St. Thomas and his teachings and determined to kill him. Knowing that he prayed in a cave on the slope of a mountain, they stood where there was a narrow opening to let in a little light, and looking through it they saw the Apostle on his knees with eyes closed, in a rapture so profound that he appeared to be dead. They thrust a lance through the opening and wounded him. When the saint sighed, they all ran away, and he dragged himself in his death agony out of the cave onto the mountain, and there died.

The Apostle Thomas, before Pentecost a pessimistic doubter, afterward became a dedicated church planter!

Matthew

Also called Levi, he was probably the most educated of all the disciples. Originally a despised tax collector, he followed the Lord's call fully, and eventually wrote the Gospel which was directed toward the Jews, trying to make them see that Jesus was their Messiah.

Early stories say that after the dispersion of the Apostles, Matthew traveled into Egypt and Ethiopia preaching the gospel. When he visited the capital, he lodged in the house of the eunuch who had been baptized by Philip.

Matthew performed miracles there, including the healing of a young woman from leprosy. According to tradition, he was beheaded by the sword in Egypt.

The words which he wrote still live and nourish.

James, Son of Alpheus

This apostle is many times confused with James, the brother of Jesus, and so few verifiable facts are available. He is believed to have founded the church in Syria. He was stoned by the Jews for preaching Christ, and was buried near the temple in Jerusalem.

Truly, the message of Christ is costly!

Simon Zelotes

Some very early writers describe Simon's ministry as follows: "St. Simon continued in worship and communion with the other Apostles and Disciples of Christ at Jerusalem; and at the Feast of Pentecost received the same miraculous Gifts of the Holy Spirit; so that he was equally qualified with the rest of his Brethren for the Ministry of the Gospel. And we cannot doubt but that he exercised his Gifts with Zeal and Fidelity. Some say he went into Egypt, Cyrene and Africa, and all over Mauritania, preaching the Gospel to those remote and barbarous Countries. He came into these Western Parts, as far as our Island of Great Britain; where having converted great Multitudes, with manifold Hardships and Persecutions, he at last suffered Martyrdom by Crucifixion."

Simon is believed to have traveled to Britain with Joseph of Arimathea. There are monuments and records in Britain pointing to their time there. Other historians believe he left Britain and preached in Syria and Mesopotamia and suffered martyrdom in Persia by being sawn asunder.

Regardless of the place, there is no question but that the zealous Simon gave his life for the Gospel of his Lord.

John Mark

Early writers record that Mark the disciple and interpreter of Peter wrote a short gospel at the request of the brethren, embodying what he had heard Peter tell. When Peter heard this, he approved it and published it to the churches to be read by his authority. Peter also mentions Mark in his first letter.

After the deaths of Peter and Paul, there is a clear tradition that John Mark went to Alexandria, a Greek-Roman city in Egypt with a large Jewish population. He brought his gospel (written in Greek) with him and may have prepared another version in the Egyptian language for natives. The dates of his entry into Alexandria are placed between 55 and 61 A.D.

One story of his ministry is interesting. When he entered Alexandria, he broke the strap of his shoe, so went to a cobbler. When the cobbler, Anianus by name, took an awl to work on it, he accidently pierced his hand and cried aloud, "Heis ho Theos" (God is one). Mark rejoiced at this, and after miraculously healing the man's injury started preaching to him. The cobbler took Mark home with him and he and his family were baptized, and many others followed.

The movement was so successful that the word spread that a man was in the city to overthrow idols. He prepared to leave the city, but before he left, he ordained Anianus and others as elders and deacons to be overseers of the congregation. When he returned after a few years, he found the church had steadily multiplied.

Again rumors spread that the Christians planned to overthrow the pagan deities and the idolatrous populace was infuriated. On Easter, 68 A.D. a mob descended where the Christians were worshipping, seized Mark and dragged him through the streets with a rope around his neck, then put him in prison. The next day the ordeal was repeated until he died. His life vindicated his testimony!

Luke

Luke was a devoted Christian, helper and companion to Paul, the apostle, who called him "the beloved physician." Through his two books (Luke and Acts), we have the earliest history of the church. According to tradition, he was crucified at the same time and place as Andrew.

Paul

Paul was not one of the original twelve disciples or part of Jesus' earthly ministry. However, many scholars believe that he was the Lord Jesus' personal replacement for Judas. He was called and commissioned directly from Heaven by the Lord, and never looked back.

According to Clement, Paul's disciple and historian (Philippians 4:3), his ministry took him to all parts of the Roman Empire, including Spain and Britain. His last letter to Timothy, written shortly before his death, reveals his thoughts on suffering for the Lord.

> *Be not thou therefore ashamed of the testimony of our Lord, nor of me His prisoner: but be thou partaker of the afflictions of the gospel according to the power of God.*
>
> II Timothy 1:8

> *If we suffer, we shall also reign with Him: if we deny Him, He also will deny us...Yea, and all that will live godly in Christ Jesus shall suffer persecution.*
>
> II Timothy 2:12 & 3:12

> *But watch thou in all things, endure afflictions...for I am now ready to be offered, and the time of my departure is at hand. I have fought a good fight, I have finished my course, I have kept the faith...And the Lord shall deliver me from every evil work, and will preserve me unto His heavenly kingdom: to whom be glory for ever and ever. Amen.*
>
> II Timothy 4:5-7 & 18

Jerome, one of the early church writers, says of Paul "He then, in the fourteenth year of Nero on the same day with Peter, was beheaded at Rome for Christ's sake and was buried in the Ostian Way, the twenty-seventh year after our Lord's passion."

Paul admonished in his writings, "Bless them which persecute you: bless, and curse not" (Romans 12:14). He instructed his readers to consider persecution an expected part of their walk with the Lord. "For unto you it is given in the behalf of Christ, not only to believe on Him, but also to suffer for His sake" (Philippians 1:29).

Persecution Through the Centuries

Jesus' prophecies, as well as the scriptural admonitions of every New Testament writer, promises that those who follow Jesus will suffer persecution. In every century since He was crucified, millions of people in every continent of the world have suffered torture and death for His Name. History documents this persecution, which many times originated in the organized institutions of the church, both Catholic and Protestant.

In our modern civilization, we may consider the concept of persecution barbaric, and refuse to accept the possibility of suffering for Him. But the promise and prophecy stands. The nearer we get to the climax of all history, the more we can expect persecution to intensify. Our commitment to Him will be tested severely. Can we say with Paul?

> *Who shall separate us from the love of Christ? Shall tribulation, or distress, or persecution, or famine, or nakedness, or peril, or sword?...Nay, in all these things we are more than conquerors through Him that loved us.*
>
> Romans 8:35-37

Group Discussion

Chapter Eight

1. Should we consider persecution as a remote possibility or expect it as part of our service to the Lord? Identify scriptures to prove your position.
2. Can you find instances of persecution in the Old Testament? Give examples. Daniel, 3 Hebrew children, Elijah
3. What was a common source of persecution against Jesus and the apostles? Pharisees
4. Who was the first person to give his life in the service of the Lord (after Jesus)? Stephen
5. Who was the first apostle to give his life? James
6. Only one apostle died a natural death. Who was he? John
7. Discuss the spiritual fortitude necessary to endure suffering and death for Jesus Christ. Are we ready for such a fate? What can we do to prepare?

Chapter Nine

Structure of the Early Local Churches

Now therefore ye are no more strangers and foreigners, but fellow-citizens with the saints, and of the household of God; and are built upon the foundation of the apostles and prophets, Jesus Christ Himself being the chief corner stone; in whom all the building fitly framed together groweth unto an holy temple in the Lord: in whom ye also are builded together for an habitation of God through the Spirit.

Ephesians 2:19-22

The Church - Ekklesia - People Called Out Together

In all the New Testament, the word *church* is never used for a building. *Church* refers to an assembly of people, and most of them gathered in homes. Paul addressed greetings to "the church that is in thy house" or similar phraseology.

Various New Testament references tell us that the disciples met together regularly on the first day of the week to break bread, worship, and bring their offerings for distribution to the poor. These home assemblies were rich in fellowship and ministry to each other. Paul gave specific instructions on the content of such meetings.

> *When ye come together, every one of you hath a psalm, hath a doctrine, hath a tongue, hath a revelation, hath an interpretation. Let all things be done unto edifying.*
>
> I Corinthians 14:26

Everyone was to be a participant in the service, with the leading of the Holy Spirit. The result in that first century was a lively, nourishing interchange which built up the body of Christ and it spread rapidly throughout the Mediterranean world. The purpose of these assemblies of called-out people was to strengthen each other for the work of the kingdom until the return of Christ. Without buildings, without seminaries, without any of the modern trappings of ministry, they learned to behave themselves in the "...house of God, which is the Church of the living God, the pillar and ground of the truth" (I Timothy 3:15). The body of Christ contained God's plan for spreading that truth to the world and they were eminently successful as long as they stayed conscious of their purpose.

> *Not forsaking the assembling of ourselves together, as the manner of some is; but exhorting*

one another: and so much the more as ye see the day approaching.

Hebrews 10:25

The Jerusalem Church

The Lord Jesus gave His direction to the apostles to be witnesses "...in Jerusalem, and in all Judaea, and in Samaria, and unto the uttermost parts of the earth" (Acts 1:8). The first local church would be in Jerusalem, with a totally Jewish congregation. At first, leadership consisted of the apostles.

When food distribution problems arose, "Then the twelve called the multitude of the disciples..." (Acts 6). The apostles dealt directly with the believers.

Following persecution, the believers "...were all scattered abroad...except the apostles." Meantime, through intervention of God to Peter and Cornelius, the Gentiles were included among the believers. This caused much dissension among the Jews. They took the position that Gentiles must first submit to the law, including circumcision, in order to be saved.

A council session convened at Jerusalem on the question, and we see that by this time the church consisted of apostles and elders governing the believers. Their decision was given by James as the spokesman. "Then pleased it the apostles and elders, with the whole church, to send chosen men... (Acts 15:22). There is no indication that James was a sole leader, as we would consider a present-day pastor. In fact, Paul later wrote to the Galatians about his early visit to Jerusalem and the apostolic leadership:

When James, Cephas (Peter) and John, who seemed to be pillars, perceived the grace that was given unto me, they gave to me the right hands of fellowship....

Galatians 2:9

The Jews had been very familiar with elders from the time of Moses in their early history. After their dispersion by Nebuchadnezzar in 5877-B.C., they built synagogues, places where they could gather together for reading the Law and for instruction. According to J.B. Lightfoot (St. Paul's Epistle to the Philippians. Macmillan & Co., 1869), "Over every Jewish synagogue, whether at home or abroad, a council of 'elders' presided."

In their meetings, there seems to have been a great deal of freedom for addressing the congregation. Any qualified person might address the assembly, but if there were a visitor present who was able to speak, he brought the message. We see an example of this custom when Jesus spoke at the Nazareth synagogue (Luke 4:16). The order of the synagogue service is given in Acts 13:15:

After the reading of the law and the prophets the rulers of the synagogue sent unto them, saying, Ye men and brethren, if ye have any word of exhortation for the people, say on.

Paul's custom was always to speak first to the Jews in the synagogues.

Other Churches Founded by Laymen or Apostles

The earliest local churches outside Jerusalem were founded by laymen who left Jerusalem after the day of Pentecost for their homes in other parts of the Roman empire. (Compare Acts 2:9 with I Peter 1:1.) Later, others were founded by those who left Jerusalem after the stoning of Stephen (Acts 8:4).

Eventually, apostles were sent out from local churches. They evangelized in new areas, then set in order each new group of believers with its own leadership (Acts 13:2,3).

Local Church Government Always Plural

Serious study of the New Testament will reveal that no single elder, bishop, pastor or deacon was ever placed in authority over the local assembly. The only time the words *bishop* and *deacon* are singular is in the listing of requirements for their service. As soon as a group of believers was formed in any locality, elders were appointed.

Another illustration of the plurality of leadership is given in Philippians 1:1. Paul addressed his letter to "...all the saints in Christ Jesus which are at Philippi, with the bishops and deacons."

Elders, Bishops, Pastors

Elders, from the Greek word *presbuteros*, indicates seniority of age and/or maturity of experience. Bishops and pastors functioned from the eldership, or presbytery. *Bishops, from the Greek word episkopos*, were overseers. *Pastors*, from the Greek word *poimen*, were shepherds, those who guide and nourish the flock.

An interesting illustration of the application of these meanings is given in Paul's exhortation to the elders of Ephesus. He had called for them to meet him in Miletus on his way to Jerusalem, and said to them all:

> *Take heed therefore unto yourselves (elders,* ***presbuteros****), and to all the flock, over which the Holy Ghost hath made you overseers (bishops,* ***episkopos****), to feed (****poimanein****, to feed as a shepherd or pastor) the church of God, which He hath purchased with His own blood.*
>
> Acts 20:28

This verse confirms that the work of overseer and shepherd were functions shared among the elders.

Paul later wrote about requirements for this office of leadership. They were to be blameless, husbands of one wife, vigilant, sober, of good behavior, hospitable, with ability to teach. They were not to be drinkers, strikers, greedy for money, covetous, or brawlers. They were to have a good report from those outside the church, to avoid reproach. One of the basic requirements was that they "rule well" their own families. If this standard was not met, they were disqualified for taking care of the house of God. I Timothy 3:1-7 summarizes these standards for overseers.

Deacons

The need for deacons, people to handle practical matters, became evident early when complaints arose about food distribution in the Jerusalem church. The apostles quickly determined that their own priorities were in the ministry of the word of God and prayer, and instructed the multitude of disciples to choose from among their number seven men to take care of the matter.

In their instructions, they specified requirements for these first deacons. They must be "of honest report, full of the Holy Ghost and wisdom." After they were chosen by the people, the apostles prayed, then laid their hands on them, dedicating them for their service.

Several years later, Paul wrote to Timothy at Ephesus, giving him high standards and requirements for deacons. They were to be serious, not double-tongued, not addicted to drinking, or greedy. These characteristics were to be proved in them and they were to be blameless. They also were required to be husbands of one wife, responsible heads of their own families.

Although the office was to handle practical matters, the deacons were to hold "...the mystery of the faith in a pure conscience" (I Timothy 3:8-13).

No Honorary Titles

Throughout the New Testament records, no leader is given a title, such as Reverend, Doctor, Father, Apostle, Prophet, Pastor, Bishop, Elder, Deacon, or Evangelist. These names as listed in scripture were designations of calling and function, not honorary titles. Only after the end of the first century, as men began to take power over other men, did these designations take a different form, giving evidence of human vanity and need for recognition.

Jesus warned his disciples about this, referring to the Pharisees:

> *But all their works they do for to be seen of men...and to be called of men, Rabbi, Rabbi. But be not ye called Rabbi: for one is your Master, even Christ; and all ye are brethren. And call no man your father upon the earth: for one is your*

> *Father, which is in heaven. Neither be ye called masters; for one is your Master, even Christ.*
>
> Matthew 23:5-10

Modern day churchmen are very particular about proper titles when being introduced or written about in the press. What a difference!

Model Church At Antioch

The Antioch church was founded by laymen who had fled Jerusalem after the stoning of Stephen.

> *Some of them were men of Cyprus and Cyrene, which when they were come to Antioch, spake unto the Grecians, preaching the Lord Jesus. And the hand of the Lord was with them: and a great number believed, and turned unto the Lord.*
>
> Acts 11:20-21

When the apostles at Jerusalem heard about Antioch, they sent Barnabas to help the new assembly of believers. He brought Saul to them for teaching. The Lord worked with the Antioch Christians and leadership developed.

> *Now there were in the church that was at Antioch certain prophets and teachers; as Barnabas, and Simeon that was called Niger, and Lucius of Cyrene, and Manaen, which had been brought up with Herod the tetrarch, and Saul... they ministered to the Lord and fasted.*
>
> Acts 13:1,2

No individual was appointed leader over the others. When Paul was in residence, he was one of the leadership,

"...teaching and preaching the word of the Lord with many others also."

They were sensitive to the prophetic word of the Lord. Agabus, a prophet from Jerusalem, delivered a message to them by the Spirit that there would be a great famine. The Antioch assembly, each according to his ability, contributed to a relief project and sent it to Jerusalem. They were a caring, generous church.

One day as the leaders were fasting and praying, the Holy Spirit said, "Separate me Barnabas and Saul for the work whereunto I have called them." After more fasting and prayer, the elders laid hands on them and sent them away. Paul and Barnabas had now become apostles – messengers, sent ones. During their journey, they preached the gospel of the death, burial and resurrection of Jesus Christ. New believers were formed into young churches.

> *When they had ordained them elders in every church, and had prayed with fasting, they commended them to the Lord, on whom they believed.*
>
> Acts 14:23

Paul and Barnabas returned to Antioch and reported back to the church which had sent them, telling them "...all that God had done with them, and how He had opened the door of faith unto the Gentiles."

Acts 14:27

The Antioch church learned how to handle controversial issues when legalistic believers visited them from Judaea. The Jews tried to convince Gentile believers that they could not be saved without circumcision. When the question could not be settled locally, the church sent Paul and Barnabas to the apostles and elders at Jerusalem. The matter was settled at a council meeting and authoritative letters written.

When Paul and Barnabas arrived back in Antioch with Judas and Silas, prophets from Jerusalem, they gathered the whole church together and read the letter to them. The people "...rejoiced for the consolation."

In summary, the Antioch church was founded by laymen preaching the gospel. When leadership was sent to help them, many people were added. Prophets and teachers developed. They ministered to the Lord by prayer and fasting. They manifested gifts of the Spirit. They exercised the ministry of giving. They sent out apostles to evangelize new areas. They did not allow controversy to divide them, but took decisive action to settle questions.

What lessons for the twentieth century are in the record of the Antioch church!

Missions, Then and Now

Compare their church planting journey with the modern missionary movement. People are dispatched to foreign countries by mission boards after spending a period of time raising funds and pledges for support. They arrive and settle into their new homes for periods of years, many times maintaining a higher standard of living than the natives, supported by money from their country of origin. How many times have natives become servants of missionaries? Instead of "equipping the saints," teaching, training and developing leadership so the natives could lead their own people, missionaries have perpetuated dependency on themselves.

Review again the description of the "missionary trip" of Paul and Barnabas in Asia Minor:

> *When they had ordained them elders in every church, and had prayed with fasting, they commended them to the Lord, on whom they believed.*
>
> Acts 14:23

If this pattern had been followed consistently throughout the generations, the world could have been evangelized by now. Proof has been found behind the Bamboo and Iron curtains. Even now in Russia and China, hundreds of house churches have surfaced from underground after years of horrible persecution. Led by the Holy Spirit, they survived and spread like the first century church. They have kept the faith for generations, proving the power of the original pattern.

If these principles were activated, the task of going into all the world could be accomplished swiftly.

By Comparison

Can you visualize a modern city with many gatherings of saints, each with their own leadership of elders? Paul sent greetings to many such churches in Rome (Romans 16). These people were not spectators, but participants in the work of the Lord. Their leaders trained and equipped them for the work of their ministry, and the church expanded outward steadily. Paul wrote to them, "...your faith is spoken of throughout the whole world" (Romans 1:8).

What a challenge for leaders and people to find the pathway back! We need some Antioch churches, with people fasting and praying, ministering constantly to the Lord, watching for the Spirit's guidance. If the Spirit directs us to send out key people from our midst, are we willing to let them go and support them on their way? Or are we unwilling to diminish our number to spread the gospel?

It will be difficult to find the old pathway to God's pattern for church structure. Many man-made methods and traditions have formed and accumulated through the years. People hesitate to make changes in patterns which have become so deeply entrenched over the centuries. Think of the possibilities!

Instructions From Early Writing - Didache 14:1-15

> On Sunday, the Lord's own day, come together, break bread and carry out the eucharist, first confessing your sins so that your offering may be pure. Let no one who has a quarrel with his friend join the meeting until they have been reconciled, so that your offering is not polluted. For this is the offering spoken of by the Lord.
>
> Appoint for yourselves therefore bishops and deacons worthy of the Lord; men who are meek and not moneylovers, true and approved, for they also perform for you the ministry of prophets and teachers. So do not despise them; they are the honorable men among you, together with the prophets and teachers.

Group Discussion

Chapter Nine

1. What is the scriptural meaning of the word "church"?
2. Where did the church assemble for worship?
3. Read I Corinthians 14:26, and discuss the atmosphere and procedure for a gathering of the people. Would such an informal atmosphere make you uncomfortable?
4. How were the earliest New Testament churches founded?
5. Discuss the government pattern of the early local assemblies.
6. What were the functions of elders and deacons (from scripture)?
7. Were people in leadership to have honorary titles? Why or why not?
8. Read about and discuss the Antioch church, comparing it with the average present-day church, in ministry sent forth, church planting, reporting back, and handling controversy.
9. Should we try to get back to that early pattern? How?

Chapter Ten

Changes During the Centuries

What happened across the years to change the structure of church leadership and the spiritual tone of the church? According to history, the second century saw the rise of "mono-episcopacy"—the rule of one bishop in each congregation. We have no clear picture of the reason this took place.

Hans Lietzmann, in "The Founding of the Church Universal," said, "If we inquire the reason of the change, the simplest answer would probably be the opinion that the concentration of power in the hands of a single person made for better leadership."

By the end of the first century, the superintendency of individual bishops (overseers) had emerged. In his "History of the Church," author Waddington states, "After all, no form of church government now existed, or could exist, accurately framed on the model of the earliest, since *that was regulated by an inspired ministry, and enlightened by extra-ordinary gifts.* The government which immediately followed that earliest was episcopal (governed by bishops)."

Clement, an early bishop of Rome who died about 100 A.D., wrote to Corinth many regulations and rules of spiritual functions. He based these largely on Old Testament procedures. Bishops and priests were to be considered divinely appointed and separate from the laity. Lietzmann says, "Here is the germ of the doctrine of divine ordination of the clergy and of its indelible character." He says that Clement's writings describe the Roman church at the end of the first century.

Dr. L.E. Elliott-binns, in his book, "The Beginnings Of Western Christendom," says,

> The process by which the bishop came to be distinguished from his fellow elders, and at last to occupy a position of authority over them and the church, can no longer be traced.

The movement toward "mono-episcopacy" gathered momentum so rapidly that by the end of the second century it was the standard pattern of church government. Each congregation was governed by a bishop, a body of elders, and a board of deacons. The gap between clergy and laity became increasingly wider. When a group became large enough, a bishop was ordained for life to minister to them. Funds of the group were committed to him. Powerful processes corrupted the original pattern and humility of leadership.

Satan can be seen at work with his familiar appeal to the "pride of life" lust. Mankind has always been vulnerable to suggestion that "ye shall be as gods."

Men became power-hungry in their climb up the ladder of authority. One historian said, "It is quite certain that bishops began very early to assume the title of 'successors to the apostles.' The roles of prophets and teachers were gradually assumed by church government. By the time of the Council of Nicaea (325 A.D.), the deacons were servants of the bishops."

Historian Kenneth Latourette wrote, "We know even less of the spread of Christianity in the second century than we do of its propagation in the first century. The vigorous, Spirit-filled, enthusiastic movement almost disappears, and we later find that the adherents of Christianity are a different group of people. The writings of the church fathers make it painfully apparent that apostasy occurred, as foretold by Paul."

New Phase

The conversion to Christianity of Roman Emperor Constantine in 312 A.D. seemed to be a tremendous, miraculous event. Christians no longer suffered for their faith at the hands of the Romans. But from that time forward, the church acquired many pagan customs. From sun worship came the name for the first day of the week: Sun Day. The birthday of the sun god, December 25, became Christmas. Candles, incense, and increased attention to the virgin Mary became part of worship. Veneration of saints and martyrs began, and images were incorporated into their church buildings and services.

After Christianity became a state religion, the Emperor was in charge of church/state relations. The Roman Emperors had always been heads of religion, even considered gods themselves. Bishops became influential, powerful men in both church and government. The church acquired property and became wealthy. Bishops were given great estates. One pagan Roman senator from the period said, "Make me bishop of Rome and I will become a Christian tomorrow."

Early Description of the Body of Christ

From an anonymous *Letter to Diognetus*, possibly dating from the second century.

For Christians are not differentiated from other people by country, language or customs; you see, they do not live in cities of their own, or speak some strange dialect, or have some peculiar lifestyle.

This teaching of theirs has not been contrived by the invention and speculation of inquisitive men; nor are they propagating mere human teaching as some people do. They live in both Greek and foreign cities, wherever chance has put them. They follow local customs in clothing, food and the other aspects of life. But at the same time, they demonstrate to us the wonderful and certainly unusual form of their own citizenship.

They live in their own native lands, but as aliens; as citizens, they share all things with others; but like aliens, suffer all things. Every foreign country is to them as their native country, and every native land as a foreign country.

They marry and have children just like every one else; but they do not kill unwanted babies. They offer a shared table, but not a shared bed. They are at present "in the flesh" but they do not live "according to the flesh." They are passing their days on earth, but are citizens of heaven. They obey the appointed laws, and go beyond the laws in their own lives.

They love every one, but are persecuted by all. They are unknown and condemned; they are put to death and gain life. They are poor and yet make many rich. They are short of everything and yet have plenty of all things. They are dishonored and yet gain glory through dishonor.

Their names are blackened and yet they are cleared. They are mocked and bless in return. They are treated outrageously and behave respectfully to others. When they do good, they are punished as evildoers; when punished, they rejoice as if being given new life. They are attacked by Jews as aliens, and are persecuted by Greeks; yet those who hate them cannot give any reason for their hostility.

To put it simply—the soul is to the body as Christians are to the world. The soul is spread through all parts of the body and Christians through all the cities of the world. The soul is in the body but is not of the body; Christians are in the world but not of the world.

Anti-Semitism Among the Church

Although the apostles and earliest Christians were Jews, gradually there crept into the church an attitude that Jews were Christ haters and therefore enemies of the church. After the church was championed by Emperor Constantine, legal discrimination against Jews increased and eventually they were deprived of all rights. As the institutionalized church spread with the Roman Empire throughout Europe, the deadly hatred of Jews spread with it and has continued in various forms through every century and in every country in the world. Even after the terrible holocaust of this century, "civilized" society is still permeated with anti-semitism. It is not surprising that Jews recoil from Christianity!

The first-century church was not anti-semitic. Paul wrote, "Brethren, my heart's desire and prayer to God for Israel is that they might be saved." He always presented the gospel first in the synagogues, then to the Gentiles. He had a deep love for the Jews. "I have great heaviness and continual sorrow in my heart. For I could wish that myself were accursed from Christ for my brethren, my kinsmen..." (Romans 9:2,3).

How could the attitude of the early church have been changed into unspeakable hatred and persecution of the Jews by an institution which claimed Jesus Christ, a Jew, as its founder? Only by rejecting the principles and Spirit of Jesus and His apostles, the foundation on which His Church is built. Where was the manifestation of the fruits of the Spirit toward the Jews: love, joy, peace, gentleness, meekness...? Small wonder that Jews cringe at the word "Christian"! Their treatment by the institutionalized church over the centuries has been an unspeakable blot on the name of Jesus Christ.

Buildings

In the process of change in the church, meeting places were removed from homes and into buildings. Even the architecture of the period reflects the increasing division between the clergy and the worshippers. Architectural sketches of Roman buildings dating from the late first century to the fourth century show that pagan shrines and palace audience halls became models for Christian buildings after they ceased worship in ordinary dwelling rooms.

By the fourth century, Christianity had settled on the pattern for its buildings from the Roman basilica, a structure used by the Romans both as a courthouse and a stock exchange. There was a rectangular hall divided into three sections by two rows of columns parallel with the longer sides of the building. At one end of the shorter side, there was a semi-circular area divided from the rest. The plan was a direct ancestor of present-day church buildings. The bishop sat on a throne in the circle divided from the rest, and the table for the Lord's supper became an altar in front of the bishop. The design effectively separated the altar and the leadership from the ordinary worshipper, and has continued through centuries.

Differences emerged in the way worship services were conducted. They continued to meet on the first day of the week to share the Lord's supper, but no longer was heard the joyful praise, worship and prayer described in the New Testament. Formal liturgies became common. Lengthy instruction was required for those desiring baptism. In the first century church, new converts were baptized immediately. Now they must be qualified by education and testing.

Extension of Government

In the latter part of the third century, a development began in which the bishop of the chief city in any province tended to become the principle bishop, or arch bishop, of that province. Later, five bishops of the chief divisions were given the title of patriarch. They governed adjacent territories, ordained archbishops and held high powers. Of these patriarchs, two evolved into rivalry between east and west, into which the Roman Empire had been divided. Rome and Constantinople were headquarter cities for these divisions.

The Roman church increased in prominence after the fall of Jerusalem in 70 A.D. Eventually the bishop of Rome established his supremacy over all the other bishops and the papacy was established. The theory of the pope's apostolic succession from Peter was made an important part of church doctrine. The church of Rome became the "apostolic see," center of authority. Bishops of other churches were addressed as sons rather than brothers.

The church shared power with the emperor. In 380 A.D., Emperor Theodosius ordered all his subjects to submit to the faith of the Pope. He took the power of executing heretics. Controversy arose among the bishops about sharing power with the emperor regarding church matters. In the late fifth century, the bishop of Rome issued the statement that the Emperor was directly subject to the Pope of Rome and should rule the Empire for the good of the church. Church and state were becoming inseparable.

The separation between clergy and laity continued to widen as the years passed. Only priests of the Roman church could give out the word, written only in Latin. Laypeople were denied access to the scriptures. The dark ages descended, but in every century there were people who tried to break out of the ecclesiastical mold and find the Lord's will, often at the cost of their lives. The wealthy and powerful church, no longer the persecuted, became the predator of those who dared to differ, accusing them of heresy. Earnest priests who had access to the written word could see the wide difference between the early church and that of their day. There were movements by those who wanted reform, but they were ostracized and eliminated by the powerful church, now backed by government. Eventually, at horrendous cost, courageous men made corrections.

Creeds and Calendars

Controversy arose because of the mystery surrounding the Godhead. Were there three separate beings, or were there three persons in one? Arguments raged on whether Jesus was of the very substance of God, or of other substance, and whether or not His blood was the blood of God. They fiercely debated about phrases, "Our God Jesus Christ," and "The Passion Of My God." In 325 A.D., the Council of Nicea stated the doctrine of the trinity in a creed which many did not accept.

Battles about the Godhead raged for several centuries between various factions of the church, involving many different beliefs and definitions. Evidence from the history of those times exhibits mankind's familiar characteristic of redefining and explaining all mysteries in his own terms.

Finally, at the Council of Chalcedon in 451, the Nicene Creed was hammered out and the doctrine of the trinity was stated in a creed which governed the church of that day and subsequently the reformation churches, continuing to the present in mainline and most evangelical denominations. Leaders who rejected the creed were judged heretics.

Differences on the subject still separate the Greek Orthodox Church, the Roman Catholic Church, and the Egyptian Coptic Church. The controversy continues to the present, even surfacing in the early 20th century after the Holy Spirit fell at Azusa Street in California. The church was split between "trinity" and "oneness" factions and the division is maintained today. One wonders why the simple scriptural statement by Paul to Timothy was not sufficient, with brethren allowing each other space to differ about how God accomplished the great mystery.

> *Without controversy great is the mystery of godliness: God was manifest in the flesh, justified in the Spirit, seen of angels, preached unto the Gentiles, believed on in the world, received up into glory.*
>
> I Timothy 3:16

By the end of the fifth century, many festivals and rites had been fixed in the church calendar. There were celebrations to honor saints, martyrs, the virgin Mary, the babies massacred at Bethlehem, the circumcision of Jesus, the ascension of Jesus, and others. Various rituals were written for specific occasions, and books of sermons for the use of clergy who could not write their own. Believers' baptism was seldom practiced, and infant baptism became the custom.

Monks and Monasteries

As the church became more worldly, there were those who responded by retreating from it, some going into the desert and wilderness to live alone, others forming communities to live together. Monks wanted to live a totally Christian life, and felt that the world hindered them. They wanted a deep communion with God, expressed by prayer, meditation and fasting, with reading of the scriptures. An important part of their work was the copying and translating of scripture. Daily tasks were shared equally. Some furnished medical treatment for the sick and relief for the poor.

From the fourth century on, monasteries were founded in North Africa, Syria, Lebanon, central and western Europe, as well as Britain, Scotland and Ireland. They became centers for spiritual life to the areas around them, with monks trying to raise the level of spirituality among the people, evangelizing and planting churches.

Pre-Reformation Reformers

The story of the church in the world between 500 and 1500 A.D. is one of continuing struggle with kings. There was expansion to all parts of the world, accumulating wealth, acquiring properties, building cathedrals, mounting crusades, establishing universities, and devising schemes to raise money, such as selling indulgences. Men who sought for truth struggled against the tide.

In the twelfth century, the Waldensians were founded by a wealthy merchant in France. Giving away all his worldly goods to follow Christ, Peter Waldo began preaching from the New Testament. There were many followers and the pope directed that they should be eliminated by inquisition and punishment. They fled and started to organize with bishops and deacons, claiming to be the "true" church. They rejected buildings, altars, holy water, liturgies, and all saints not named in the New Testament. They spread throughout central and eastern Europe and were still going strong during the fifteenth century, although many paid with their lives.

In the fourteenth century, John Wyclif of England became the enemy of the church because of his anti-clerical position. He believed that the real Church was God's chosen people and did not need a priest to mediate for them. Before he died, he translated the Latin Bible into English. His followers were called "Lollards." Possible meaning of the word was "mutterer" or "mumbler". (Did they speak with tongues?) The Lollards paved the way for Luther's reform.

In Czechoslovakia, Jan Hus was influenced by the works of Wyclif. He emphasized scripture as authority and defined the church as the body of Christ, with only Christ as its Head. He was burned at the stake in 1415. The ministry of Wyclif and Hus had attacked the very foundations of the medieval church and papacy. The corrupt church was threatened.

One of the biggest factors in the reformation was the invention of the printing press. About 1445 Gutenberg of Germany developed movable metal type, and the first complete book printed was the Bible, in 1456.

The Protestant Reformation

In 1517, Martin Luther of Germany, after a long spiritual struggle and study of the book of Romans, came to a new understanding of the nature of God and justification by faith. He published "95 Theses," a protest against indulgences. He did not plan it to be a call to separation, but pointed to the unscriptural practice of selling penances. He did not intend to leave the church, but wanted changes. However, he was excommunicated by the pope in 1520 and outlawed by the Emperor. For twenty-five years he published books and papers exposing the errors of the Roman church, spending much of his time as a fugitive.

Luther's controversial movement was called "Protestant" and eventually gave way to three main divisions: the

"Lutheran" in Germany; the Calvinist ("Reformed") in Switzerland, France, Holland and Scotland; and the Church of England ("Anglican"). The main principles of the Protestant Reformation were (1) that only Scripture contains God's word for man, (2) that salvation was by grace alone, and (3) that every believer is a priest. They rejected church traditions which had accumulated through the centuries, and the movement spread rapidly.

An important influence on the Reformation was that of William Tyndale, who spent his life translating the Bible into English. He fled from England to Europe to do his work, and completed the New Testament, of which about 90% is included in the King James Version. Before he could complete the Old Testament, he was seized in Brussels in 1535, strangled and burned.

There were other giants of reform in the sixteenth and seventeenth centuries: Calvin, Bucer, Beza, Zwingli, Bunyan, the Puritans and the Anabaptists. Some were imprisoned, some gave their lives.

The Anabaptists were fought by both Catholic and Protestant churches because they wanted to go back to the roots of Christianity in the New Testament. They preached that there are no sacred *things*, such as images; no *holy places*, such as church buildings; no elevated *saints*—all who belong to Christ are saints; no *sacred person*, such as a priest, to serve communion. They served each other the elements of the Lord's Supper. They refused to baptize their infants, but preached adult water baptism. They believed that every member had a responsibility to communicate the gospel in word. Their test of any theological statement was always the life and doctrine of Christ and the apostles.

The Catholics put the Anabaptists to death by fire, and the Protestants drowned them (mocking baptism). Their spiritual descendants are the present-day Mennonites.

Catholic Response to Reformation

The Protestant movement caused the Catholic church to lose large areas of Europe, but it also caused a "Counter-Reformation" among many in high places. The Roman church faced the truth of Martin Luther's allegations and began to reform the church from within. Organizations and societies, such as the Jesuits, were formed to strengthen the church through moral improvement. The papacy itself was changed and higher caliber men made attempts to end corruption. The Council of Trent was convened in an effort to salvage and maintain political power. This Council reinforced the major Catholic doctrines: transubstantiation, clergy celibacy, purgatory, indulgences, papal authority, worship of Mary. The result strengthened the Catholic church, but left in place many non-apostolic practices and beliefs.

The century after Luther's revolt brought about many religious and political wars between Catholics and Protestants. These affected Germany, France, Holland, England, Sweden, Denmark, and were finally settled in 1648 at the Peace of Westphalia. Meantime many were fleeing to other countries, including America. There was both Catholic and Protestant expansion into other countries during this period.

According to historian LaTourette, neither the gospel carried by the Pilgrims into New England or the missionary efforts of the Jesuit priests on the west coast was that of the original early church. It had become "another gospel."

The Great Awakening

In the 1730's, a fresh move of the Spirit was tangible, both in England and in the North American colonies. All but one of the thirteen colonies had been founded by Protestants who rebelled against religious oppression. There were Calvinists, who believed that no one is saved who is not "elected." There were Congregationalists, formed by merging Puritans and Separatists. There were Presbyterians from Scotland and Ireland, who governed by presbyters with a Moderator as leader. The first Baptists were organized by Roger Williams, formerly a Separatist, among the English and Welsh in Rhode Island. At the beginning of the eighteenth century, large numbers of German Lutherans came to Pennsylvania at the invitation of William Penn. Other German groups, Moravians and Anabaptists, came as well.

After this varied mixture of people settled into life in America, they seemed to forget the conditions that brought them, and became preoccupied with their new lives and new country. Church attendance became nothing more than a ritual observance, and a Boston minister of the early eighteenth century reported, "We are at this time fallen into as dead a sleep as ever." But revival was coming.

A German Reformed minister, Theodore Frelinghuysen, arrived in America and was shocked by the deadness of his denomination. In 1720, he began evangelizing and the revival spread to the Presbyterian churches. In 1733, Jonathan Edwards began preaching in Northampton, Massachusetts and an awakening began there.

In England, the Anglican church had declined and moral standards of the country had declined with it. Two or three clergymen of the church began to call sinners to repentance. Their devout preaching brought results throughout the land, and even into Wales, with thousands gathering to hear them. George Whitefield was converted in the Welsh revival and immediately began preaching in England, with converts in London. He recruited lay preachers to travel.

In January of 1739, some of the leaders of the revival effort gathered in a "love feast." John and Charles Wesley were present, as well as George Whitefield. John Wesley later wrote in his Journal,

> About three in the morning, as we were continuing in prayer, the power of God came mightily upon us insomuch that many cried out for exceeding joy and many fell to the ground. As soon as we were recovered a little from that awe and amazement at the presence of His majesty, we broke out with one voice, 'We praise Thee, O God, we acknowledge Thee to be the Lord.'

The work of the Holy Spirit that night was felt in the ministries of John and Charles Wesley, whose "societies" revolutionized England within ten years and spread to America through immigrants from Ireland.

Even Scotland, whose Presbyterians had become lifeless and torn with strife, was touched by the Spirit's working. One pastor had preached for over thirty years without effect. Then he began a series of sermons on the new birth, and wrote two years later, "While pressing all the unregenerate to seek to have Christ formed within them, an extraordinary power of the divine Spirit accompanied the word preached."

From *"A Faithful Narrative of the Surprising Word of God."*

By Jonathan Edwards

There was scarcely a single person in the town, old or young, left unconcerned about the great things of the eternal world. Those who were wont to be the vainest, and loosest; and those who had been most disposed to think, and speak slightly of vital and experimental religion, were now generally subject to great awakenings. And the work of conversion was carried on in a most astonishing manner, and increased more and more; souls did, as it were, come by flocks to Jesus Christ. From day to day, for many months together, might be seen evident instances of sinners brought out of darkness into marvellous light, and delivered out of a horrible pit, and from the miry clay, and set upon a rock with a new song of praise to God in their mouths.

This work of God, as it was carried on, and the number of true saints multiplied, soon made a glorious alteration in the town; so that in the spring and summer following, anno 1735, the town seemed to be full of the presence of God: it was never so full of love, nor of joy, and yet so full of distress, as it was then. There were remarkable tokens of God's presence in almost every house. It was a time of joy in families on account of salvation being brought unto them; parents rejoicing over their children as new born, and husbands over their wives, and wives over their husbands.

George Whitefield arrived in New England in 1740 and embarked on a six-week preaching tour which brought about a great change in the colonies. Boston crowds were so large that no church would hold them and he began preaching in the open air. This continued for months, and penetrated the churches in all the colonies.

Overall, the Great Awakening was a sovereign move of the Holy Spirit which had long-lasting effects in many nations. The spiritual effect contributed indirectly to the American revolution. Missionaries were sent out. Social justice was aroused. The fight to banish slavery was begun. Prison reform was activated. Through Wesley's "societies" clothing and food were distributed to the poor. It is worthy of note that God worked not through organizations, but individuals, to accomplish the work.

The Civil War in America during the 1800's brought about divisions between the northern and southern sections of the country and of each denomination. While empires rose and fell in Europe, the United States was undergoing a survival test.

After the war, Christianity followed frontier expansion west with campmeetings, circuit rider preachers and revivals.

Missionary Expansion

At the beginning of the eighteenth century, an industrial revolution was under way in England which brought social evils with terrible factory conditions and child labor. This period saw the rise of Sunday schools, conducted by Christians so children who worked in factories all week could receive schooling on Sundays.

The Salvation Army began its ministry which continues to the present.

By the middle of the eighteenth century, the Jesuits had founded missions along the coast of California. Protestant efforts followed the trading companies sent out from Europe. The devout Moravians in particular began missions in at least ten countries. David Zeisberger, one of the Moravians, followed the Iroquois and Delaware Indians and was beloved by them. David Brainerd of Scotland worked among the American Indians, and although his life was short, his writings have inspired others even to the present.

Home missionary agencies began to form along denominational lines. Christianity became represented around the world by social missions and cultural transplanting.

Evangelism receded. Missions in the last two centuries have "Christianized" all parts of the world, reinforcing denominational structures, creating systems of education, transplanting western culture along with commerce. They have created dependency on the part of the native churches, instead of developing indigenous leadership within them. They have tried without success to solve the problems of poverty, social injustice, racial discrimination, and materialism, which abound world-wide.

Two wars in this century and the development of trade and industry have changed patterns all over the globe. At one time in history, Christianity was altogether the "white man's religion." Now people of every race and in every nation consider themselves Christian. Bible translation and increased literacy have placed the scriptures within the reach of many people around the world.

Where was God in this Picture?

When we read the depressing history of Christianity over the centuries, we wonder how God looked at it. Did He recognize and bless the great "Christian" empires which joined church and state?

Careful research of history shows that God still intervened in the affairs of men, but did not follow the rules, regulations and patterns which men put in place. He worked by His Spirit through individuals.

The record shows that in every century since Pentecost, His Spirit has been active in men. His gifts have been manifested in prophecy, tongues, healings, faith, wisdom, and knowledge. Lives of individuals from the first century to the twentieth show that the Holy Spirit did not abandon humanity, even though the visible "church" wandered far away from Him. Those who reached out in hunger for Him received answers to their cries, regardless of the religious labels on their church doors.

As we approach the twenty-first century, it is difficult to be optimistic. The church, far from being the light in the world which Christ intended, is but one factor in an extremely complex world situation. Many times through the centuries the Lord has intervened through those who cried out to Him. Will He do so again?

When Jesus urged His disciples to pray and not to faint, He said, "Nevertheless, when the Son of man cometh, shall He find faith on earth?" (Luke 18:8)

What is our answer?

Group Discussion

Chapter Ten

1. Discuss the changes which took place over the centuries and differences in the way the local churches were governed, how they gradually became ruled by one man instead of elders, the way services were conducted, and other changes which occurred.
2. What significant event took place in 312 A.D. which seemed to be very favorable to Christianity? What was the actual effect?
3. Discuss the record of anti-Semitism in Christianity.
4. From meeting in homes, they graduated to buildings which gradually became more luxurious and elaborate. How did these buildings affect the gathering of the people?
5. How did church and state become so powerfully intertwined for centuries, and what was the effect?
6. Consider some of the controversies which erupted in those early years, and their effects.
7. What is the significance (if any) of the Christian calendar?
8. Discuss the fact that down through the centuries, there were always those who wanted to go back to the original pattern. What usually happened when they tried?
9. In light of history, can we be optimistic about the future of the church in this world?

Chapter Eleven

"...Stand...See... Ask ...and Walk...."

Stand...and See

We have been searching the scriptures for God's intent for His Church today. Our purpose is not to generate controversy but to identify truth.

The question: is the present system working as Christ intended for His Church to function? When Jesus gave final orders to His apostles, the commands included others:

> *Go...teach all nations...teaching them to observe all things whatsoever I have commanded you...*
>
> Matthew 28:19,20

Included in those final commands was promise of empowerment to believers:

> *Repentance and remission of sins should be preached in His name among all nations, beginning at*

> *Jerusalem...Behold, I send the promise of My Father upon you: but tarry ye in the city of Jerusalem, until ye be endued with power from on high.*
>
> Luke 24:47, 49

> *These signs shall follow them that believe; in My name shall they cast out devils; they shall speak with new tongues; they shall take up serpents; and if they drink any deadly thing it shall not hurt them; they shall lay hands on the sick, and they shall recover.*
>
> Mark 16:17,18

His final instructions concerned the message, their mission, the empowerment with supernatural signs witnessing their words. The commission should not have ended with the first century—He promised to be with us in the work until the end of the world. The work should still be going on!

Alexander R. Hay, in his *New Testament Order For Church And Missionary*, p. 127, writes:

> The fact is that the Apostles, fulfilling the ministry which God gave them, laid a complete and perfect foundation for the Church, both as regards structure and doctrine. A careful and unbiased study of the New Testament will make it abundantly clear that a full and detailed revelation is given regarding the structure of the Church and that all the congregations planted in apostolic times were organized in accordance with that pattern.

The church of Jesus Christ was given all things needed to do the work He expected us to do—the orders, the plan, and the power to implement them. As we "stand and see" the church today, we have fallen far short. Over the centuries, as we have learned, the church has become an institution instead of an organism. Both the leadership and the laity must take responsibility to make changes in this generation.

This can be difficult. In a personal vein, during the writing of this book a church in the local area split, the pastor leaving with part of the congregation. Those left were trying to hold together with great difficulty. One of the members told me, "We feel so lost, so abandoned...." I described the work I was doing in preparation for this book and gave them a draft, explaining that their's would be an ideal "lab" situation for proving or disproving the thesis. The response? "Oh, this is scary! We're looking for a new pastor." They had been conditioned for so long as a passive audience that they could not conceive that the Lord would raise up leadership from among them.

So if changes take place, they must come from both leadership and the people. Leadership must recognize that their calling is to equip the saints for *their* ministry. The people must accept that God does not call an ordained few, but expects all to exercise their gifts in ministry.

Did Christ really want an elder in each assembly elevated to operate as an individual chief executive officer, as the pastoral position has become? Did He want it to be a profession comparable in the community to doctors and lawyers? Some denominations consider the requirements for a pastor to involve administrative skills, psychological counseling skills and of course he must be a good performer in the pulpit.

In contrast, read Peter's admonition to the churches of Pontus, Galatia, Cappadocia, Asia and Bithynia:

> *The elders which are among you I exhort, who am also an elder, and a witness of the sufferings of Christ, and also a partaker of the glory that shall be revealed:*
>
> *Feed the flock of God which is among you, taking the oversight thereof, not by constraint, but willingly: not for filthy lucre, but of the ready mind;*
>
> *Neither as being lords over God's heritage, but being ensamples to the flock. And when the Chief Shepherd shall appear, ye shall receive a crown of glory that fadeth not away.*
>
> I Peter 5:1-4

Is it possible for people to be led by a group of elders rather than by an individual? Some would consider it to be "governing by committee," with every decision subject to wrangling and opposition. Keep in mind that this was *God's* plan.

Our Lord set in place a *plural* leadership and expects us to be willing to follow His plan. What if elders can't agree with each other? Peter answers that question in writing to the elders:

> *...Yea, all of you be subject one to another, and be clothed with humility: for God resisteth the proud, and giveth grace to the humble. Humble*

yourselves therefore under the mighty hand of God, that He may exalt you in due time.

I Peter 5:5,6

Jamie Buckingham, a well-known minister now deceased, wrote that in making decisions with his fellow elders, no action was ever taken without unanimous agreement. If they were not together on a decision, they went to their knees before God until the Holy Spirit made known His will in the matter. That takes being "clothed with humility"!

Down through the centuries, people who questioned the existing church order and wanted to go back to scriptural principles were persecuted by the people who claimed to be God's appointed church.

Ask For The Old Paths

What should we ask for?

People who want to serve the Lord in His harvest field need elders operating as apostles, prophets, evangelists, pastors and teachers who will train and equip them for the work of their ministry.

They need help in learning to be disciples and to disciple others into the kingdom with the gospel. Where is the leadership which will teach and exhibit the fruits and gifts of the Spirit in the process of training others? Who will lead in prayer and fasting for these gifts?

Where is the leadership which will prepare people for coming persecution? Many sermons are preached on the rapture which will take us all away from the terrible conditions to come, but few are preaching on the command to "Occupy (keep busy with profitable work) till I come." The Lord has left His servants with capital to work with until His return. What will His leadership show Him at His return?

Walk Therein

Paul wrote to the Corinthians (I Corinthians 16:15):

> *I beseech you, brethren, (ye know the house of Stephanas, that it is the firstfruits of Achaia, and that they have addicted themselves to the ministry of the saints,) that ye submit yourselves unto such, and to everyone that helpeth with us, and laboureth.*

What high praise for Stephanas' household, and what a privilege to submit to such leadership! Surely the flock would prosper and increase under such ministry.

Paul gave guidelines for the gatherings of the saints in I Corinthians 14. He told them that when they assembled together, everyone should have something to share with the others. One might have a psalm which had blessed him since they last met. One might have a word of doctrine from the Lord. Two or three might have a tongue if there were interpreters.

Someone might have a revelation to share. Two or three might prophesy, subject to judgment of others. The purpose of prophecy was "that all may learn, and all may be comforted" (Romans 14:31). He emphasized the importance of the Holy Spirit's leading:

> *Let us wait on our ministering...on teaching...on exhortation...giving...ruling...showing mercy.*
>
> Romans 12:7,8

Those following the leading of the Lord will not be promoting themselves, monopolizing time instead of sharing time with others.

Can you see from the apostle's instructions how enriching such gatherings could be? There would be such an atmosphere of worship, love and caring for one another that when they separated, each would feel strengthened and blessed for having been there. They would be equipped and empowered to witness to unbelievers, strengthened to face persecution.

There are groups of people meeting for prayer and Bible study, hungry to know more about eternal things. There are groups who have been abandoned by pastors searching for more lucrative fields.

Young evangelists who feel the "GO YE" call should also research the original plan and think of the possibilities in evangelizing in a new area, making disciples. Then, when a nucleus of people has accepted the gospel and been trained in scriptural principles, leadership could be formed and set in order to mature and reach out to others.

Does it sound too difficult for our twentieth century expectations and dreams of mega ministries? Do we want to be gratified with our careers, with men's recognition of our efforts? Read Paul's resume of accomplishments in Philippians 3:4-6, and his conclusion: "But what things were gain to me, those I counted loss for Christ."

If we gain a perspective from the scriptures that ministering according to *God's Word* should be our objective, we will submit our will to His and labor faithfully.

We will recognize that we are *all* to be preachers in our own area of influence, spreading the gospel message, bringing others to the Lord for discipleship. We can ask the Lord to identify from His elders the apostles and prophets to minister to us, with the evangelists, pastors and teachers who will equip and train us for our ministry. We can covet the best gifts, as we are instructed to do, keeping in mind that they are to be exercised in love. We can be strengthened to face inevitable persecution, since we know that they persecuted Jesus, and we can expect it. Jesus' admonition to His disciples in that first century was:

> *...Lift up your eyes, and look on the fields; for they are white already to harvest. And he that reapeth receiveth wages, and gathereth fruit unto life eternal: that both he that soweth and he that reapeth may rejoice together.*
>
> John 4:35,36

That command given to His first disciples extends to us who are part of His end time Church. There is even more urgency for us because of the time factor. But if we put in place the ministry provisions made for us back in the first century, we can expect the same increase recorded then, because our God is the same today as yesterday.

Group Discussion

Chapter Eleven

1. Discuss the pros and cons of making changes in systems which have been in place for centuries.
2. Even though the present systems are not what Christ intended, is it necessary to make changes?
3. Does the informal, sharing, gathering of the people described in the New Testament seem appealing, or do you prefer the more formal "platform oriented" service?
4. Are the hazards of false doctrine more of a possibility with the New Testament format?
5. What would be the best method to incorporate the original ways into our gatherings?
6. What is the most important consideration of these studies?

COMING...

UNTO THE LEAST OF THESE

By Abbie Tuttle

A book dealing with a vast mission field of millions incarcerated in America under the county, state and federal prison systems.

SHOULD THE CHURCH BE CONCERNED?

DO THESE COME UNDER THE GREAT COMMISSION?

WHAT SHOULD WE DO?

Watch for announcement of publication.

Check your local Christian bookstore for additional copies of *ASK FOR THE OLD PATHS* or order direct:

ANGELIA PUBLICATIONS
10632 E. Jefferson Road
Osceola, IN 46561